CONTENTS

Thank you! Don't Forget to Pick Up Your Free Gifts

Introduction: Why I Write About Narcissism

Chapter 1: From Surviving to Thriving

Chapter 2: Discovery

Chapter 3: Identifying Toxic Family Relationships

Chapter 4: Understanding Codependency

Chapter 5: ACON (Adult Children of Narcissists)

Chapter 6: The Gatsby Defect – The Narcissist in Love

Chapter 7: Identifying Toxic Friendships

Chapter 8: Identifying Narcissistic Personality Disorder

Chapter 9: Gaslighting – a Narcissist's Go-To Manipulation Tactic

Chapter 10: Dealing with Overbearing Narcissists in Your Life

Chapter 11: Understanding Narcissistic Rage and Narcissistic Injury

Chapter 12: Being a Narcissistic Supply

Chapter 13: The Ideal Source of Narcissistic Supply (What Narcissists Want)

Chapter 14: Detoxify Yourself and Your Life

Chapter 15: Where You Go From Here (Limits, Schimits)

Chapter 16: Forgive, Don't Forget (The Letter)

Chapter 17: The Opinions That Matter, and the Ones That Don't

Chapter 18: Insecurity and the Hard Times

Chapter 19: Why It's So Hard to Walk Away from a Narcissist

Chapter 20: The Toxic Love Drug

Chapter 21: Considering No Contact

Chapter 22: Taking Back Your Power

Chapter 23: The End of the Toxic Relationship

Chapter 24: Redefine Yourself After a Toxic Relationship
Chapter 25: The Miracle Question Takes You to the Next Level

INTRODUCTION: WHY I WRITE ABOUT NARCISSISM

A lot of people wonder why I so often write about narcissism and toxic relationships. The short answer is that as a certified life coach and author, I am also someone who has survived narcissistic abuse in my own relationships.

That's why this particular topic is so close to my heart. Because I know how it feels to doubt yourself, to feel almost like you're going crazy under the extreme pressure of a toxic relationship. I know how it feels to, in desperation and as an attempt to survive, go completely numb and wish you could remember who you wanted to be – who you're supposed to be. To break under the overwhelming energy of a toxic narcissist.

Some people (rightly) call them emotional vampires, and that is exactly what they are. Their need for "narcissistic supply" causes narcissists to actively "suck all the air out of the room" – or at least, to suck any and all emotional energy from their victims, who are left deflated and a shell of themselves.

As a life coach who has been involved in narcissistic relationships in my life and not only survived, but who currently thrives, I feel compelled to share my experiences, at least to the extent that they are valuable to my fellow survivors. Plus, being a former journalist and a seasoned researcher, it's in my nature to learn about (and write about) things that concern me.

It's just how I roll.

I started writing about this topic for my own healing – I needed to understand exactly what I'd been through and why it had happened.

So, as I worked on healing myself and on detoxifying my life, my healing manifested itself in many ways – some of which were honestly shocking to me.

The first was the dismissal and redefinition of a particularly toxic family relationship I was stuck in for way too long. While this may have been a significant change in my life, it isn't one you can see when I walk down the street.

Just like the psychological and emotional injuries that are a result of being in a toxic relationship with a narcissist, you can't tell that a person is stuck in a narcissistic relationship unless you happen to be a personal witness to the behavior of the narcissist.

As a result of both the shame a narcissist's victim can feel for not standing up for him or herself as well as fear of the narcissist's reaction if they do, the victim often feels like they have no one to turn to for help. They're too embarrassed to ask and the narcissist is too concerned with appearances. And since narcissists tend to isolate their primary victims, the victims are especially unlikely to reach out for support.

Like I mentioned, to the narcissist, the victim's energy is like life blood. This makes us the "source of narcissistic supply," and that role is both exhausting and soul-crushing. It feels like a trap you can never escape, and it steals your very identity.

But there IS hope, and there are real, actionable steps you can take to survive and even thrive. I am here to help you see that you're not alone, and that you become strong enough to reclaim your life, your power and your Self. I am here to share this hope and this knowledge with you so that you too can become the powerful person you ae meant to be, and so that you can create the life you truly deserve.

That's why I write about narcissism and toxic relationships so often. As I continue my own healing journey, I feel compelled to share what I learn with my readers. After all, my life's mission is to help you become the best possible version of yourself–to create the life you want. And in order to do that, you've got to heal your WHOLE self.

So, no more putting band-aids on this problem, alright? Stick with me. The healing is about to begin. Are you ready?

CHAPTER 1: FROM SURVIVING TO THRIVING

The first time I wrote publicly about narcissistic abuse in toxic relationships was in September of 2010. That was when I wrote a post about how to identify toxic family relationships, and at the end of that post, I promised to come back and explain how to deal with the situation. When I wrote that, I assumed I would have figured it out by the time I wrote that post.

What I didn't mention in that post was that I was dealing with a toxic family situation of my own which had culminated into an event of painful betrayal that affected me on an emotional level so deep that I was physically ill for weeks afterward.

It wasn't with anyone in my household, thankfully, but it did involve a couple of extended family members I had been very close to at one time. One of them had been toxic for many years, but because of the nature of the relationship, I had continuously "turned the other cheek." I tried and tried to make it work and I now realize that I developed a shockingly codependent relationship that I couldn't even recognize while immersed in it.

The other family member involved had been a ghost in my life for the previous 15 or so years, only showing up on rare holidays and special occasions, and the act of betrayal on this person's part shook me to the core because it was completely unexpected.

How I Handled My Toxic Family Situation

So, as I often do when I experience challenges in life, I wrote my way through it. If you're familiar with my work, you know I'm not a poet and I don't do flowery (very often) so I did what I do - I did some research and wrote a logical, fairly informative article on how to identify toxic family members. Though I wanted to share with my readers how to handle such a situation, I stopped there because, at that point, I had only identified my toxic family members–I didn't actually know how to deal with them.

Over the next several months, I would have a lot of realizations. Since then, I have connected the dots, so to speak, of my own experiences. I have come to understand those toxic relationships on a whole new level, and in fact, after many hours of reflection and emotion, I have managed to forgive the people involved–at least within myself. I needed to do that for the sake of my own sanity.

What's Happening Now with the Toxic Relationships

As for the relationships with my toxic family members, you might be surprised to know that I haven't repaired them. Considering the events that took place, I don't know that those relationships can be repaired at this point, and I don't think it would be healthy for me to try.

I remain "no contact," meaning I don't actively have any involvement with them at all. It wasn't easy, but it was worth the effort in so many ways.

For example, now that I am not dealing with these people on a day-to-day basis, I don't have to try so hard to see the positive side of things. The weight of the relationships has been taken off my chest, and I can breathe. There is a new lightness in and around me that I'm not sure I've ever felt before. In some ways, I can be grateful for the situation, because in dealing with it, I found a level of strength within myself that I never knew was there.

What's Happening Now with Me

It would be easy for me to sit around and feel sorry for myself and to cry over the things that happened, but I choose to hold my head up and keep smiling. I prefer to live in the present moment instead. I don't want to focus on the negative and the past–I want to live in the now and look expectantly to the future.

So that's what I'm doing. I'm enjoying my relationships with my immediate family, a few extended family members, and those people who have become family through love (and not blood). I'm following my passion, rocking my career and exploring the new-found freedom that comes with healing–and generally all is well in my world. These days, I've decided, I'm writing my own ticket.

I'm Still "Human"

Don't get me wrong, I still have feelings of sadness about the situation and the lost relationships. I have those moments of self-pity when I wish things could have been different, just like probably anyone who has dealt with a toxic family member or situation.

I did attempt to reunite with my toxic family members a few years ago, but it was short-lived. It seemed that while I had changed, my toxic family members had not. I realized that it wasn't possible to have a healthy relationship with them and I sadly made the choice to go permanently no-contact. It was the right thing to do, and I have no regrets.

Staying Positive is the Key

If I sit around worrying about what happened and constantly rehashing the events in my mind, I draw more of that type of negativity toward myself. On the same note, if I focus on feeling love and gratitude for the wonderful people, things and events in my life - guess what? More of that comes my way.

So, when those feelings of sadness or depression or self-pity creep up, I intentionally change my mind and focus instead on all of the awesomeness in my life.

If you're in a similar situation, you should try intentionally focusing on the positive too—and on changing your mind if the negative thoughts do creep in. It might feel forced at first—but once you get the hang of it, it comes naturally. And the more you focus on what's good and right in your world, the more power you give to those things. The less you think about the things you don't want in your life, the less of those things you'll draw toward yourself.

I don't know about you, but I'll take happy and positive over negative and soul-sucking any day.

CHAPTER 2: DISCOVERY

I was sitting at my desk bawling one day (after a phone call with a rude scheduler at my doctor's office) when the doorbell rang. I wiped my eyes, but I didn't even get up. I figured it was one of the many neighborhood kids who practically lived there during the summer.

But when my son yelled, "Mom, some lady's at the door asking for you!" I jumped up. At the door stood a beautiful young woman with a concerned look on her face.

"My name is Jane and I'm with child protective services," she said. Noticing my tear-stained face, she said, "Oh, are you okay?"

I nodded and briefly explained what had happened with the rude lady on the phone, and then asked her how I could help her.

"Uh, we got a call from someone who said your children are being neglected," she said, almost apologetically. "I'm here to investigate."

I felt the blood rush to my face and my heart was suddenly pounding. I have never been perfect, but I'm a good mom and everyone who knew me knew how much I love my kids.

"What? I don't understand," I said, feeling dizzy. "Who would do that?"

She told me that someone had called saying that my kids didn't have food to eat and that there was trash and junk all over my house. And that my oldest child was reportedly raising the others while I just left them alone all the time. Of course, none of this was true and the problem was quickly resolved. But what that event revealed would change my life forever – and not in the ways one would expect.

The Betrayal That Would Change My Life Forever

Once she had determined that I was not the neglectful, abusive person someone had claimed I was, and that my children were, in fact, safe, healthy and happy, I asked the social worker if I could read the report that had been taken when this supposedly anonymous person had called the CPS hotline.

She agreed, and as I read through the report, I was shocked at how bold and unfounded the claims of neglect and abuse actually were. And then it happened. I read the line: "Her oldest son is raising his brothers and sisters."

I felt the wind knocked out of me. I knew in that moment exactly who had made that call. I knew without a doubt. I knew because I had heard that same language a thousand times growing up.

It was my own mother.

Not only did my oldest child only have one brother and one sister (not plural brothers and sisters), but my mother had said over and over again throughout the years: "I had to raise my brothers and sisters."

I couldn't breathe. My head was spinning. My heart had dropped to my stomach and I felt like I was going to throw up.

How could she do this to me?

I knew she had never approved of literally anything I did. I knew she didn't like me as a person.

But I had believed her when she said she would always be there for me. I had believed her when she said family was forever, and that no matter what happened, she'd always have my back.

I had believed that, though she'd gossip and lie about me to the family and probably her friends, when it came to the big important things, she would never betray me. I never, ever thought she would call CPS on me. Not in a million years.

What Led to the Betrayal

I'd always had a strained relationship with my mother, to say the very least. We had conflicting personalities. She believed I should be a carbon copy of herself, and I could never quite make that happen. Anytime I tried to go "rogue" and do something outside of the lines she had drawn for me, I was doing it to "hurt her," she thought and said. If I had an opinion or a thought or a feeling or a belief about something, it was quickly poo-pooed, brushed off, minimized.

Growing up, this led to my feeling completely and totally worthless. The one thing I wanted from my mother was validation. I wanted her to be proud of me for something that was all me. I wanted her to say I was good, that I mattered. That I was important.

But she couldn't. Instead, she would just look down her nose at me and judge me. When it came to me and who I was becoming, she would alternate between feeling shame for having a daughter like me, and rage that I wouldn't or couldn't stay within the lines that she had drawn for me.

Fast-forward several years. I was on my second marriage and my third child. My youngest was a year old, my oldest, the only child of my first marriage, was 11.

I had been arguing with my mother for several weeks. It seemed that she wanted to take my oldest son on vacation with her to California to visit my brother. I had agreed, because even though I couldn't always afford such experiences, I didn't want to take them away from my child if she was offering.

The thing was that this was the first year that my little family could afford a "real family vacation," and we had planned a trip to Florida, where we were going to show our kids the beach for the first time.

I told my mother that as long as her trip was after ours, it would be okay. She agreed, and things seemed like they'd be okay.

But a few days later, she called me while I was getting the kids out the door for school, and my husband out the door for work. She said that she was buying plane tickets for their California trip and needed to know RIGHT NOW if the dates she had chosen would be acceptable.

I told her that I would check my calendar and call her back after I got everyone out the door, 15 minutes later. She said she couldn't wait. She needed to know right now!

I reminded her that I had told her my dates before, and she could just refer to those. But she said she couldn't remember the dates, and in the moment, neither could I.

So I asked my husband about the dates she mentioned, and he said it was fine with him as long as it was after our trip. I explained this to my mother, and she said, "Fine, I'm buying the tickets now."

But when I went and checked my calendar 15 minutes later, I realized the dates she had chosen were the week before our trip had been planned. We had already paid non-refundable deposits on the condo we rented on the beach and it had been set in stone.

I quickly picked up the phone and called my mother to ask her to reschedule and was quickly informed to "get over myself" and that she would not reschedule. When I tried to ask her to do so and explained my reasons (that I wanted to be the one to show my son the beach for the first time), she acted like that was the dumbest thing she had ever heard and brushed it off before completely losing it.

She started screaming obscenities and insults at me and before long, hung up the phone on me. Moments later, the phone rang, and it was my dad, who had raised me since I was six. He informed me that I was a complete piece of shit who didn't deserve anything and that I had horribly upset my poor mother, who was only trying to be nice. He said he had never really liked me and had only put up with me "for her sake," and that this was too much.

I can't remember what I said to him after that, but I am sure it wasn't very nice. I remember a lot of crying, angst and emotional devastation.

I decided in that moment to pull away from my parents in order to preserve my sanity. But since I didn't want to take experiences away from my son, I allowed him to go on the vacation, and I allowed him to go to church camp with my mother and brother that same month. I still maintained my distance from her and kept it "all business, all the time." I'd only discuss the business of her being a grandmother to my child (and I didn't say "children" here because she still to this day hasn't bothered to be much of a grandparent to my youngest two, save for one or two half-hearted attempts early in their lives).

Too-Small Shoes

The day before my son was due to go to church camp with my mother and brother, we were getting together his suitcase and supplies for the week. He was being his usual self, preferring to play video games instead of doing what we needed to do. He haphazardly gathered up the clothing needed for the week at camp and when I asked him where his shoes were, he said he didn't know.

I had just bought him brand new name-brand running shoes the week before, and he refused to find them. Instead, he found a pair of shoes that was a little too small and kind of falling apart.

I told him he would be miserable in those shoes all week. That they wouldn't support his feet and that they would hurt. He told me to stop worrying so much, that they would be fine. He reminded me that the camp papers said to bring old shoes you didn't mind ruining.

I told him I didn't care if he ruined the shoes, but I wanted him to take his new ones. I wanted his feet to be comfortable and I didn't want people to think I didn't buy him shoes when he needed them.

He brushed me off and said it would be fine, going back to his video game.

In frustration, I said, "Fine, if you would rather play video games than spend five minutes looking for your shoes so you can be comfortable at camp, that's your choice. But I promise you'll regret it by Tuesday."

He told me he knew what he was doing and again said he'd be fine. And at that moment, I decided to let him learn his lesson. Maybe with sore feet for a week, he would finally realize that sometimes, being prepared is better than playing a video game.

Right or wrong, that was my parenting decision at that moment. And it would come back to bite me in a way I would never have expected.

See, while he was at camp, he complained to my mother and brother that his shoes hurt his feet. They took pity on him and zipped into town to buy him a new pair, and when they arrived to drop him off at the end of the week, they said nothing about the shoes.

But I noticed them right away and asked about them.

They both looked down their noses at me and informed me that his shoes were too small, and all torn up. I explained what had happened, thinking they would understand and even be on my side. I offered to pay my mother for the shoes. She declined.

After that, I continued to have what I would now call "low-contact" or limited contact with her, focusing only on the business of her grandparenting my son.

The Final Disappointment

Weeks later, I called my mother excited because I had received the proof copy of my first book.

"Mom," I said. "I can't believe it! My name is on the cover! This is such a big deal!"

She said nothing about the book and instead told me she was very busy and had to go, as she had been doing for awhile now.

I was disappointed that she wouldn't be happy for me. I wanted her to be proud of me, as I always had, and as she did as she had always done.

I felt that old familiar lump in my stomach. But I tried to push it down and celebrate with my kids instead.

Later that day, I had to call my doctor about an issue I was having – and after hearing some upsetting news, was sitting at my desk in my converted garage-office area, sobbing quietly so the kids wouldn't hear me.

And that's when the doorbell rang.

The Truth Comes Out

My heart was pounding as my eyes raced along the words of that CPS report. There it was in black and white. In addition to the outrageous lies and assumptions they had made, there was the language used – and then, there was the mention of the shoes. I was in shock. I could not believe this was happening.

I would learn later that it was even worse than I thought. She had "turned" my brother on me. He had fallen for the lies and made-up stories she told him about what a terrible mother I was. She had "whipped him up into a frenzy," as she was prone to saying, and made him believe I was neglecting and abusing my children.

It seemed that, along with my brother, with whom I believed until that moment I had a positive relationship, she had created a made-up story about how I was parenting my kids, who my kids WERE and how my household ran.

The social worker interviewed me, my husband, and my children, and she looked around our house. She checked to see that we had food in the fridge and pantry, she looked in our drawers and our closets. She looked at the kids' bedrooms and in our back yard.

Finding nothing wrong, she closed the case the same day.

She put her hand on mine and told me not to worry. She explained to me that there are a lot of folks who waste the department's time with what they call "revenge calls." And, she explained, this seemed to be one of those.

Something Broke Inside Me That Day

That was the day I went no contact with my mother, and it's the day that my whole life changed. For my entire life, I had felt obligated to her. I felt like I needed to keep her happy, and that I wasn't ever good enough because I couldn't be whatever it was she thought I should be. (I'll leave it at that because to explain the details would take hundreds of pages.)

She had betrayed me – THEY had betrayed me, in a way that I could never have imagined that they would. It completely changed everything for me. It woke me up and fast.

At the very moment I realized that my own mother had willfully done this to me, attempted to have my children taken from me (or at least risked that), I almost physically felt something break inside of me – that cord of obligation that had always been there and had always caused me to bend to her will – it broke.

In one single moment, I lost the ability to care how she felt. And more than that, I lost the fear of her. She had always intimated that if I stopped doing what she wanted, or refused her too many times, she would abandon me and then I'd have no one. I lived in that fear for 35 years.

A Moment of Clarity Launches a Movement

Before that day, I thought that even if she was a hard person to deal with, and even if she rarely ever validated me or attempted to understand me, and even if she didn't seem to care about my feelings, at least she had my back when it came to my family.

I could never have imagined (nor would I have believed) that she would stoop so low to hurt me. I cannot even come up with the right words to describe the way I felt – it was almost like the time I was running in the dark as a kid and tripped over a branch, knocking the wind out of myself. I felt like I had the wind knocked out of me.

But then, I got mad. Well, not just mad. After years of being a people-pleasing, self-hating codependent, I was filled with blistering, blinding rage.

Soul-twisting, screaming, ugly rage that comes up from deep inside and nearly forces you to take swift action. The kind that causes you to get crystal-clear on what you want and what you deserve real quick. I was filled with what I now know is justified rage. I was indignant. And in that very instant, I was done. I went no contact and since the one failed attempt I made to reconnect several years ago, I have not looked back.

But it wasn't so simple. Even though I officially ended contact in that moment, it took a long time before I could see that there would be a silver lining to all of this.

Going no contact was instinct for me in that moment. I did not fully understand why I was doing it, but I just knew it had to be done. At that moment, as with many other moments in my life, my decision was based on my desire to protect my children. Not myself. As usual.

But I felt myself changing somehow.

This event launched a period of reflection that started a whole movement in my life. Suddenly, I could see everything clearly – and as it turned out, I wasn't giving myself enough credit. I had spent my life trying to be something that someone else wanted me to be – but I couldn't be that thing because it wasn't, well, who I was. This led to me questioning literally everything I believed, thought, felt and did up to this point.

Later, I would also discover that my first husband had been a toxic narcissist as well. It shocked me because he had seemed to be almost the polar opposite of my mother. But that's when I learned that there were different kinds of narcissists and that their toxic behaviors could manifest in different ways.

Seeing Clearly

In time, I started to see things more clearly. As the psychology of it all started to make more sense to me, I started creating some real positive change in my life.

I recognized and eliminated a couple of key relationships – very toxic ones that I couldn't even see until after I had this moment of clarity. It was the beginning of my personal evolution, and while I wouldn't wish this experience on even my worst enemy, I have come to be grateful for it, because it led me to my life's work, and it led me here, in this moment, to you.

While I had been professionally blogging for a few years about work stuff, and while I was a journalist by profession, I needed a creative outlet as well. That was why I had a personal blog where I wrote about what I was going through and ways I was handling it. I wrote about how I was managing to deal with the "difficult" people in my life – and how I was changing my perception in the process.

But back then, I didn't understand what was happening in my life – not really. It took me several years to realize that I was also blogging for thousands of other people just like me – people who were survivors of narcissistic abuse. At that point, I didn't even know what narcissistic abuse really was, nor did I recognize myself as someone who was dealing with it.

(These days, someone tells me nearly every single day that I have helped them in some way – often that I've saved their lives. Just because they read or watched or heard me say something that resonated with them or woke them up. It's an amazing gift that comes along with the kind of work I do.)

But what so many of these amazing people don't know is that, inadvertently, they have saved ME. See, it was through my work blogging that I started sort of trying to figure out what was really wrong with me – and as it turned out, it led me to discover NPD abuse and C-PTSD.

Writing My Way to Sanity

I've always written my way out of trouble. This began with a pink diary with a little lock on it at age 6, continued with handwritten journals into my 20s and eventually, led me to blogging in my early 30s.

My first blog-therapy (as I like to call it) experience was with weight loss blog on BuddySlim – a website that was dedicated to diet and exercise back in the early 2000s. This was a community blogging site, and it provided some much-needed validation for me at the time. It took my own "journal therapy" idea to a whole new level – I was getting valuable feedback from my peers – and WOW that was a beautiful thing! Heck, I eventually lost 100 pounds!

Fast-forward a few years, and I had decided to become a stay-at-home mom. I love my kids so much! But to be honest? That worked for about 10 minutes before I decided I needed some intellectual stimulation. This, of course, led me, a journalist by trade, to blogging professionally.

I founded my first personal blog, In Pursuit of Fulfillment, in 2006. That site was originally created to allow me to share my own journey to personal fulfillment in an effort to connect with and help others who were on similar paths.

As the blog and the community around it grew, I grew right along with them. Over the years, In Pursuit of Fulfillment became Project Blissful, which included the original content and new content that was at least half weight-loss and maintenance focused – but also mindset and perception-focused. I had learned that choosing your perception was a big and important thing to understand in weight loss – and that a lot of the problem, for me, was a huge lack of self-love.

This grew my community and I later wrote a book with the same title after having lost the weight. During this time, I found myself researching my situation with my mother.

After digging through many psychology books and reading many research papers, I realized what I should've known all along: I had been dealing with narcissists who were abusing me in my relationships. More than one – and boy, had it started early!

QueenBeeing is Born

This led to the development of QueenBeeing.com, the site you may recognize among all of these. Perhaps I'd have rethought the name if I had realized that a quarter of my audience would be male.

Either way, while I was originally writing about all sorts of personal development stuff, eventually, I recognized that my best work was about narcissistic personality disorder, narcissistic abuse recovery, and the related topics. I knew this because anytime I wrote on these topics, people flocked to my blog – and they started reaching out to me, asking for my personal help with their situations.

Having realized what I had gone through was a huge breakthrough in my life – it literally opened doors for me that I didn't even know existed! I found myself having realization after realization about what I believed, what I thought and what I knew to be true. It turned out that, at age 35, I had to rethink everything I believed about myself and even the world around me.

Narcissistic Abuse is Subtle, All-Encompassing and Soul-Crushing

Narcissists have this way of shoving their twisted perceptions right into our brains – and this is especially true when we're dealing with a narcissistic parent, but also when we're in any sort of long-term relationship with a toxic person.

This creates some major issues for us as we develop and grow in our lives. We learn to doubt who we are, what we are – what we see and believe. We are taught that we're not good enough – and after enough brainwashing, we start to believe it.

I remember thinking I wasn't even a real person.

Thankfully, life is so much better these days. I've gone no contact with the narcissists in my life. I'm married to my best friend and have a beautiful family. And I spend my days doing what I love – what I really care about: helping survivors of narcissistic abuse find their way to freedom – and to their true selves. This is truly one of my biggest (and most divinely driven) mission in life.

As I always say, I can't complain!

Every day, I learn something new, something that makes my life just a little bit better. I have learned how to use intentional thoughts and to choose my perception in order to bring about positive changes in my life, almost without fail. It really is "all in your head."

That's why it's my mission to teach others what I know to be true: you really can create the life you want.

The truth is that life can be beautiful, and you can have everything you want– it all starts within you. Your perception builds your world, and the best part is that you get to choose how you perceive literally every thing and situation in your life. You can be happy, right now.

You truly can enjoy the journey to personal fulfillment, personal development and true passion—AND you can look and feel amazing while you do it. How? You start with YOU – start with yourself.

Take care of your body, take care of your soul. Nurture the real you and introduce him or her to the world. Be comfortable in your skin, and in your place in the world. Take your spot, take it now, and the universe will take its cue from you.

CHAPTER 3: IDENTIFYING TOXIC FAMILY RELATIONSHIPS

As we travel along the road to realizing our personal bliss, most of us encounter obstacles along the way. Sometimes, the obstacles are within our own selves, and other times, they come from external sources. Toxic relationships, in particular, can be an extreme source of stress and discord in our lives–and can even lead to our own lives spiraling out of our control.

You might be aware that I have published many articles and videos on toxic friendships and romantic relationships. But what if the toxic person in your life isn't a friend, but a family member?

How do you know if you have a toxic family relationship?

In general, if you feel like you're being emotionally, physically, spiritually or otherwise abused, manipulated or mistreated by any family member on a regular basis, there is an element of toxicity. These family members can include your spouse and other nuclear family members, but also extended family such as parents and in-laws, siblings, aunts and uncles, grandparents and other relations.

Your toxic family member may over-criticize you or openly judge you for your personal choices, or they may be a little sneakier about it by gossiping or telling lies about you (or your choices) behind your back. Some family members may take it to a whole other level and actually attempt to wreak havoc in your life or even to control, destroy or alter your nuclear family, domestic situation or other outside relationships.

Other Signs of a Toxic Family Relationship

Overstepping Boundaries–Psychological boundaries are defined as perceptions or beliefs that people hold in relation to their social group memberships, including but not limited to families, as well as their own identities and overall self-concepts. In part, boundaries help us to distinguish ourselves from other people–you know, that thing which separates "I" from "We." Boundaries also help us define how we are linked together within our families and extended families. Toxic family members often have trouble with boundaries. That is, they will often feel entitled to involve themselves in your life on an unhealthy level. They may try to make you feel responsible for their emotions or their circumstances, blame you for things that you have no control over or try to control you and your choices.

Unfair or Unrealistic Requirements–Toxic family members generally have different beliefs or perspectives than you when it comes to things like trust, responsibilities, money, time and attention. They may become angry if you don't do as they wish, even if it doesn't directly affect them–but especially if it does. For example, if you are unable to attend a family gathering, a toxic person might try to make you feel guilty or simply stop speaking to you.

Double Standards–Many toxic family members hold tightly to their own double standards. For example, they may expect you to keep their secrets or "have their backs" when other people gossip negatively about them, but they can't or won't offer you the same courtesy.

Manipulation–Toxic family members are master manipulators–and they will deny it if you call them on it. They will use every manipulation technique at their disposal in order to control you. They may cry, scream, argue, beg– anything they can think of to get you to do what they want, even if what they want isn't what's best for you. And, if the first technique doesn't work, they'll often move down the list.

Co-Dependence and Enmeshment

Enmeshment and co-dependency are two unfortunate byproducts of toxic family relationships. In a co-dependent relationship, one or both family members involved are psychologically influenced or controlled by the other– or they may need that other person to help fulfill their own needs or even to feel whole. While the term "co-dependent" was originally coined by the Alcoholics Anonymous recovery group, it has since been adopted by psychologists and other mental health professionals.

"A co-dependent person is one who has let another person's behavior affect him or her, and who is obsessed with controlling that person's behavior," says author Melody Beattie, in her book, *Codependent No More*.

Enmeshment goes hand-in-hand with co-dependence. When you are enmeshed with another person, it means that you depend on that person to define your identity, your sense of being good enough or worthy of having good things in your life, your overall sense of well-being and even your own safety and security. Or, to put it more clearly - you are enmeshed when you can't feel like a whole or satisfied person without the approval or presence of another person.

Being enmeshed with a toxic family member is unhealthy for all involved–it isn't compatible with being an individual. Enmeshment takes away your personal power and the ability to manifest your true desires.

CHAPTER 4: UNDERSTANDING CODEPENDENCY

Codependency can be an unhealthy side-effect of a toxic relationship with a narcissist, but what does "codependency" really mean? What are the signs of codependency? What does a dysfunctional family have to do with codependency? And how do you stop being codependent?

When you hear someone use the word "codependent," often the first thing you think about is someone who is in a relationship with an alcoholic or drug addict. That's because the term was developed specifically for this kind of relationship – initially.

What is the origin of the term codependency? The term was developed by therapists who observed that family members often took on the psychological defenses and survival behaviors of the alcoholic or drug addict, thereby extending the disease from the individual to the entire family.

What is the definition of codependency?

"Codependency" is defined as an unhealthy relationship where partners are overly reliant on one another. As a result, a dysfunctional pattern of living and problem-solving develops between the two. This is a learned behavior, most often learned in childhood, meaning it is often passed from parent to child over the course of many generations. Psychologists consider it both a behavioral and an emotional condition that affects your ability to have healthy relationships.

Who is affected by codependency?

Originally, the term was used to refer to the family members of alcoholics and drug addicts. Today, we understand that codependency also affects people in toxic relationships. Codependency begins in the family, meaning that it can affect any type of relationship, but the codependent personality is developed in childhood due to family dynamics.

How Codependency Develops in the Dysfunctional Family

Dysfunctional families are more common than most people realize. While the dysfunctional family deals with regular conflict, blatant (and more subtle) misbehavior, they often appear "normal and healthy" to outsiders. In reality, many kids in dysfunctional families deal with physical or emotional neglect and in some cases, psychological and/or physical abuse from parents, step-parents and older siblings, often on an ongoing basis.

Why does a child from a dysfunctional family become a codependent adult?

We develop our understanding of the world and our place in it in childhood. Our parents reject, ignore or neglect us, causing us to feel like we don't matter, or like we aren't seen or heard. When we are made to feel unimportant, invisible and unworthy, we begin to see ourselves this way.

We're not validated and are in fact invalidated by our dysfunctional families. This leads us to become unhealthy, codependent adults. And, if we don't heal ourselves, we can end up raising codependent, dysfunctional children, who may then continue the cycle with their own children.

Bottom line: kids who grow up in a dysfunctional family become codependent adults because dysfunction feels normal to them, so they subconsciously seek it out or attract it to themselves. Then, they pass it along to their children, who in turn, do the same. That's why a total personal evolution is required to fully overcome codependency – and to potentially protect future generations from being dysfunctional.

Codependency in Toxic Relationships

As you might expect, this is also a common phenomenon among people who are in relationships with narcissists. This is because the narcissist has such unreachable standards in any relationship that the "supply" is treated as an extension of the narcissist's self, when it's convenient – and as nothing, when it's not.

Does that make sense? Both the narcissist and the codependent have no sense of self – so they need to have a connection to someone else (the narcissistic supply) in order to sort of siphon off their energy and personality.

How do you know you're in a Codependent Relationship with a

Narcissist?

When two people have a very close relationship, it's natural and mentally healthy to depend on each other for certain things. However, if one of you is toxic, abusive (mentally, physically or otherwise), controlling and/or overly neglectful of the other person in the relationship, this can lead to codependency.

If you're the victim in this situation, you lose sight of who you are, in order to please only the other person, the relationship can become very unhealthy. One of the most troubling relationship elements is codependency.

Still not sure you're dealing with codependency? Ask yourself the following questions – and be honest when you answer them. This will help you understand if you've fallen into a pattern of codependency in your relationship.

- **Are you afraid to express your true feelings to your partner or family member?** If you notice you often hold in your feelings because you're worried about how this person will react, that's a sign the relationship is not as healthy as it could be.
- **If you do express feelings honestly, do often end up feeling guilty?** Maybe you find yourself thinking, "I shouldn't have said anything… it just made matters worse" after you've shared your thoughts with your partner or family member.
- **Do you spend a lot of time trying to do everything for this person?** If you're carrying out many tasks for someone that could easily be done by them, you might be caught up in a dysfunctional, codependent relationship. These chores might even be preventing you from living your own life.
- **Are you overly cautious asking for help from your partner or family member?** In a healthy relationship, partners and family members freely and regularly ask one another for help with various things that come up.
- **When you do ask for help, how does your partner or family member react?** Hopefully, they are open and willing to help you out whenever you ask. However, if you're codependent, you might not feel comfortable with asking or with their inevitably negative response.

- **Do you find yourself feeling hurt or angry because your partner or family member doesn't notice your needs?** While you try to take care of everything, you find yourself disappointed that your partner or family member never seems to really see or care about what's going on with you. You feel like you're continuously waiting for them to recognize your needs, but they rarely do, if ever.

- **Do you believe you can't have a friendship independent of your relationship?** Either because of the constant demands of your partner or family member or because you are too emotionally exhausted, you don't have time or energy to maintain a friendship.

- **Do you have hobbies and activities to enjoy separately from this person?** To maintain a healthy individual identity, you need to cultivate your own hobbies and interests, separately from the relationship. If you don't or you feel like you can't, it could be a sign of codependency.

- **Do you try to control things to make yourself feel better?** Because you feel like you're walking on eggshells, you don't want to upset your partner or family member. Therefore, you take steps to control situations however you can, and sometimes, those steps might be unhealthy for you.

- **Would you describe this person as needy, emotionally distant, or unreliable?** These qualities often draw in people who are seen as "caretakers" and often, people who are empathic – as in they FEEL the feelings of the people closest to them. Relationships between those of us who want to take care of people by nature and toxic, needy people can be a really toxic combination that nearly always launches a codependent relationship.

- **Do you often find yourself trying really hard to get things exactly right?** You feel like maybe if you get things perfect, this person will be happier, more satisfied, and less angry, upset, or annoyed with you. If you feel this way, your relationship is likely codependent.

- **Do you trust this person?** If can honestly answer yet, maybe your relationship is not codependent – or maybe you're not able to see it yet. I trusted my mother until the moment she betrayed me. Even though I knew she didn't seem to "like" me very much, I believed that she loved me. If you often feel this person is not telling you the truth about something, there could be codependency in your relationship. On the other hand, there may be just some trust issues you might want to resolve.

- **How is your health as it relates to stress?** Often, people involved in codependent relationships experience health issues that might be related to stress like asthma, allergies, out-of-control eating, chest pain, and skin disorders. If you're worried about your health, please see your doctor as soon as you can.

Can you relate to some of these points? If so, you might really be dealing with codependency. But don't worry too much.

The good news is that if you believe you're in a codependent relationship with a narcissist now, you can begin changing your behavior right away. This can lead you to discover (or rediscover) a healthy sense of who and what you are – and that is what will lead to your healing from this abuse and pain.

CHAPTER 5: ACON (ADULT CHILDREN OF NARCISSISTS)

"The typical adult from a narcissistic family is filled with unacknowledged anger, feels like a hollow person, feels inadequate and defective, suffers from periodic anxiety and depression, and has no clue about how he or she got that way." ~Pressman and Pressman, The Narcissistic Family

Living with a narcissist can be difficult for anyone - but growing up in the care of one can affect your life in very significant ways. For example, most narcissists use a horribly painful sort of manipulation called gaslighting – it's the worst kind because it messes with your mind in ways you'd never expect. This is especially true for the children of narcissists, who can't get away from it and have no concept of what "normal" actually looks like from the inside.

Many children of narcissists spend their whole lives thinking "I wasn't good enough," and wondering if their mothers/fathers/other caregivers could and would always be better than they.

The faces of parental narcissism

"Narcissists have two faces — the one they wear in public, and the one they wear at home," according to LightHouse.org. "Only those close to the narcissist have any idea there is more than one face. And the narcissist's children know best of all, because children – those who have the least power – are the ones the narcissist allows him or herself to be the least guarded around."

So, kids of narcissistic parents are forced to pretend in public that all is well– all the while knowing that when they get home, things will be different. In some cases, they dread going home because the difference is so significant.

"Narcissistic parents lack the ability to emotionally tune in to their kids," writes Karyl McBride, Ph.D. "They cannot feel and show empathy or unconditional love. They are typically critical and judgmental."

Many kids of narcissists express the same kind of frustration: everyone thinks their narcissistic parent is a saint–the best person ever, McBride says, noting that "while at home their children suffer in silence with their parent's tantrums, disinterest and put-downs — this is clearly NOT the most wonderful person if you truly know them — not even close."

What are you trying to prove?

"Because of its insidious nature, gaslighting is one form of emotional abuse that is hard to recognize and even more challenging to break free from. Part of that is because the narcissist exploits one of our greatest fears – the fear of being alone." ~ From my book on overcoming gaslighting and narcissism, *Take Back Your Life*

When you're raised by a narcissist, you might spend your life trying to prove something–maybe that you have value. Whether you choose to become "perfect" or you go to the other extreme, your narcissist will likely actively discredit everything you do, say or feel. You might start to think you don't matter–and that you're not even all that "real."

I remember believing that nothing I felt or wanted was as real as whatever my narcissist felt or wanted. Even during a recent interaction, I expected a third party to instantly assume I was wrong because of lifelong conditioning.

Your thoughts, feelings and opinions are rarely, if ever, validated by a narcissistic parent–and when they are, it's only when you happen to feel the same way your narcissist does. This continues into adulthood for most children of narcissists.

Once you realize that, you might even start to tell yourself that your opinion is, in fact, always consistent with the narcissist's. It causes so much less trouble, and you're treated to the illusion of approval if you comply.

But the fact we must remember is that narcissists can't feel empathy–so they aren't really capable of changing their opinions. They believe they can't be wrong.

You get to write your own story

"…all narcissistic parents fail to treat their children as authentic individuals who have their own unique characteristics and needs," says LightHouse.org. "Narcissists treat their children as mere blank screens for projecting their own internal 'movies' onto."

You see, by always acting like my thoughts, feelings and opinions had no value (like she was "better" than me), my narcissist inadvertently made me feel worthless, not good enough, not important.

Until the moment I went no contact once and for all, anything I said to my narcissist that is contrary to her opinion was met with an eye-roll and a wave of dismissal.

But this is nothing new, and in some ways, it's not this person's fault. Growing up, every idea I had was, according to what I saw and heard, eye-roll-worthy, and very little of what I said or did was treated as valuable. Still, today, she doesn't respect me or my opinions, but now, I understand that she doesn't need to–I don't need to have her approval to be good enough.

This is a fairly textbook kind of narcissistic manipulation, according to my research over the years.

"Adult children of narcissists typically describe their parents as mean, phony, self-absorbed, judgmental, dishonest, immature and manipulative," says LightHouse.org.

Evolution is inevitable

The healing process for an adult child of a narcissistic parent is a long and sometimes difficult one–but it's worth the effort. Whether you walk away completely, or you choose to limit your relationship to only necessary interactions, you would be wise to give yourself the space you'll need to evolve and grow into the individual you're meant to be.

As the adult child of a narcissist, you're bound to have picked up a few (or more) thoughts, feelings and beliefs that aren't really your own. So, once you get your space, start there: figure out exactly what you believe, and what you don't. You might be surprised to find out which beliefs or thoughts you've been carrying around for all these years for no reason.

The next step is to begin to embrace the fact that you're an individual who has value. Your thoughts, feelings and experiences are legitimate and worth hearing about–and you are just as good as anyone else.

Therapy and/or coaching can help you heal

Sometimes, our wounds are too deep to heal on our own. While some of might kill ourselves trying to live up to that impossible standard our narcissistic parents set and others choose to go the opposite direction, all of us can benefit from learning to do better for ourselves.

McBride points out that effective therapy for adult children of narcissists has three primary steps.

- Understand the background, history and diagnosis
- Deal with the feelings related to the history
- Begin to re-frame and view life through a different lens.

"The Wild West philosophy of 'get over it already' does not work with this recovery program, nor do simple affirmations or initial cognitive behavioral work," McBride says. "This specialized recovery involves cleaning up trauma first and accepting that your parent is not going to change. The change will be within you."

CHAPTER 6: THE GATSBY DEFECT – THE NARCISSIST IN LOVE

If you've ever read *The Great Gatsby* or seen any version of the movie, you probably remember the main character, Jay Gatsby. At first glance, the way he loves Daisy seems beautiful and passionate. It's the kind of love every woman wishes for – but it doesn't last long.

The Gatsby Defect: Defined

When I first read *The Great Gatsby*, I was a freshman in high school, and I didn't really "get" it – a lot of the allusions to sex, drug and gambling went right over my head. I read the book from a very innocent and naïve perspective.

And maybe, from that 14-year-old perspective, it was easy to take a lot of things at face value that I shouldn't have. (Or, maybe I was reading an edited version of the book). But I also didn't understand something else back then: Gatsby was a raging narcissist.

He was honestly a textbook case.

So, when I recently caught the Leonardo DiCaprio version on cable, I saw it with a whole new set of eyes (and from a whole new perspective, now that I've had a lifetime of experience under my not-so-virginal belt). That's how I finally saw it.

I've written or years on narcissism and the effects it can have on relationships and on the people who live in these toxic situations. And, as I've mentioned, I've survived a few of those relationships myself.

So when my adult self saw the movie and got a grip on some of the more adult themes, it was more clear to me. I realized what I was seeing. Jay Gatsby was a raving narcissist.

While he is an extreme example who "did it up" bigger than most narcissists – and was probably among the most grandiose of the bunch, his weakness and insecurity shone through like a beacon – especially in his private moments – just like any other narcissist.

And, just like his fellow toxic narcissists, Jay Gatsby was just another grown-up child who really never thought he was good enough (and because "good enough" was an unclear, self-defined concept, it couldn't ever actually be achieved).

As a result of those insecurities and underlying issues, those who would point out any faults or issues Gatsby had were made to pay dearly for their indiscretion. Gatsby seemed to think it was all about ownership; he wanted to possess people. He saw them as objects in his collection of beautiful things.

That's how narcissists roll – they dehumanize the people who love them the most and they turn them into sources of narcissistic supply. They need this supply to feed the endless hole that is their starving ego. Without it, the narcissist becomes enraged, unstable and even more unpredictable than usual. When things don't go the way they want them to or expect them to, the narcissist makes sure that no one around them is happy or able to enjoy their time.

If you've ever been in a sexual or romantic relationship with a narcissist, you might already understand that they often seem to be more interested in sex and various other kinds of instant gratification types of pleasure (food, shopping or spending money, drugs, etc.) than actual emotional intimacy.

In fact, narcissists (and those diagnosed with narcissistic personality disorder or NPD) "are more likely to philander and dump their partners than people who view important parts of a relationship," according to psychologist Ilian Shrira.

"Narcissists have a heightened sense of sexuality, but they tend to view sex very differently than other people do," said Shrira, in a 2006 study. "They see sexuality more in terms of power, influence and as something daring, in contrast to people with low narcissistic qualities who associated sex more with caring and love."

That's why some narcissists tend to bounce from one relationship to the next – and most often, the relationships don't last long, and they don't involve much emotional intimacy.

"Even when they're in a relationship, they always seem to be on the lookout for other partners and searching for a better deal," Shrira said after the study. "Whether that's because of their heightened sexuality or because they think multiple partners enhance their self-image isn't entirely clear."

Narcissists typically have an inflated sense of their own level of importance and they expect people around them to admire them and cater to them.

They often appear to have an overblown ego and can be very charming if they choose to be. According to authors Steven Carter and Julia Sokol in their book *Help! I'm in Love with a Narcissist*, there are ways to know if your significant other is a narcissist. They are as follows.

- It feels like you're the one doing most of the work in the relationship.
- Your partner does things to sabotage the relationship and prevent it from moving forward – but doesn't want to let you go either.
- Your partner might have a history of troubled relationships and/or addictions.
- Your partner has episodes of excessive and often unjustified anger – and sometimes infidelity – and he/she somehow makes it all your fault.
- You feel emotionally exhausted, often completely drained, by how hard you have to work to make or keep your partner happy.
- The relationship is mostly focused around your partner's interests and selected activities. When it's not, there will be an ugly argument or outburst.
- You feel controlled or manipulated by your partner's moods to the point that you might feel like you're walking on eggshells all the time, a slave to his or her whims.
- You might find yourself covering up, explaining or apologizing for his or her behavior.
- Your partner might make one-sided decisions that impact your safety and well-being.
- You might feel unsafe by some of the actions your partner takes.
- Your partner will refuse to see your good intentions, always blaming you for every situation, always making you admit you're wrong, even when that's not the case.
- You sometimes find yourself desperately trying to remember the

times when your partner showed love for you, acted like you could do no wrong—often this is in the early parts of the relationship.

Does any of this ring true for you? If so, you might be dealing with a toxic love relationship as well. This isn't uncommon – many of us who grew up in toxic family situations find ourselves in relationships with toxic people as adults, too. It feels normal to us somehow. But stick with me, here. We're getting to the healing part soon. Next, let's look at toxic friendships.

CHAPTER 7: IDENTIFYING TOXIC FRIENDSHIPS

"Don't walk in front of me, I may not follow. Don't walk behind me, I may not lead. Just walk beside me and be my friend." ~ Albert Camus

Toxic family relationships and toxic love relationships will destroy you, but what about toxic friendships? Are those even really a thing? I mean, after all, a friend isn't technically someone you're stuck with, right? Friendships are voluntary, aren't they?

Well, let's discuss that. When we're talking about a true friend, we're not talking about someone who toxic. But what is a true friend, in your opinion?

Everyone has a slightly different definition–but for our purposes, let's define a true friend as someone who is there for you when you need him or her, someone you trust, someone who makes you feel good.

Probably you have great conversations, share interests and support one another in your everyday lives. But what happens when a friend turns out to be "not so good" for you, if the friendship becomes toxic?

What is toxic friendship, anyway?

"The phrase 'toxic friend' is pop psychology," says psychologist Dr. Jenn Berman. "I would say it's someone who, after spending time with them, makes you feel bad about yourself instead of good; someone who tends to be critical of you — sometimes in a subtle way and sometimes not so subtle; a friend who drains you emotionally, financially, or mentally, and they're not very good for you."

How can one truly identify a toxic friendship?

It can be difficult, especially if you have been close to the friend for a long time. If you suspect that a friend is (or has become) toxic, ask yourself the following questions:

- How do you feel after spending time with or speaking to this person? Do you feel good and positive (for the most part) or do you find yourself worrying, stressing or obsessing about some aspect of the visit or call?
- Are you afraid to tell your friend about some aspect of your life for fear of how they'll react or fear of being judged harshly?
- Do you sometimes find yourself avoiding contact with the person or ignoring their calls? Does your friend consistently "forget" about your plans or cancel at the last minute?
- Does your friend actively insult or offend you on a consistent basis?
- Do you find yourself feeling uncomfortable or bothered by your friend's life choices, behavior or moral conduct?
- Do you feel comfortable bringing up concerns about your friendship with this friend?
- Does this friendship benefit you?
- Do you trust this friend, really trust him or her?

These are just a few questions to get you started. In general, your friends should be an asset to your life, not a detriment.

Does someone in your life seem to be more of a hindrance than a help on your journey to personal bliss?

If so, it may be time to reevaluate your choices.

CHAPTER 8: IDENTIFYING NARCISSISTIC PERSONALITY DISORDER

Toxic family, love and friend relationships can take a toll on anyone who has to deal with them, especially when mental illness or personality disorders are involved.

Any sort of mental illness or personality disorder among family members, especially left untreated, can cause stress and discord in the family, but sometimes, the affected person doesn't even realize there's a problem.

This is especially the case with narcissistic personality disorder, generally because a narcissist, by nature, sees no fault in him/herself. And he/she's not capable of it, either.

So how do we go about identifying narcissistic personality disorder?

If you've ever dealt with someone with narcissistic personality disorder (NPD), you'll know exactly what I mean.

"They tend to exaggerate in an immensely obvious way – as people, they're unusual in their personality," says clinical psychologist Jillian Bloxham. "It becomes very evident when a person is narcissistic."

Healthy self-esteem is important for everyone, but some people develop an over-inflated sense of self-importance that leads to the belief that other people's feelings, thoughts, and beliefs have no relevance. This is the first sign many people recognize in a person who suffers from NPD.

NPD is a tricky condition because often, narcissists don't even realize anything is wrong–so identifying narcissistic personality disorder can be a challenge–but mostly for the narcissists themselves.

In general, narcissists are known for their sense of personal entitlement that causes them to expect people around them to cater to their every desire, to anticipate their every need and to respond post-haste in fulfilling them.

"It is good to think highly of yourself – but for these people, it is out of control," says personality disorders expert and consultant forensic psychologist Kerry Daynes. "It has gone off the scale."

Do you know a narcissist?

Narcissists tend to be caught up in their own lives, their own personal worlds. This means that in general, they have no time to consider the feelings, thoughts or needs of the people around them. Rather than offer sympathy if you are dealing with pain or frustration, they'll just share some of their own with you (which, of course, will be far more serious than your own).

While a narcissist may appear to be an upbeat, happy person to outsiders in his or her life, people who know them intimately are likely to see a whole other personality. This can manifest in several ways–but a primary marker is that they are unable to empathize with those around them, and they consistently blame others for problems they've caused.

Since narcissists tend to see other people as objects or possessions, they cannot fathom it when they are not obeyed or catered to. If the person is a friend or acquaintance, the narcissist may just discard them and pretend they don't exist–but if it's a family member, things can get more serious.

For example, the narcissist may try to pressure the family member into conforming to his or her wishes, and if that doesn't work, additional and potentially life-altering steps may be taken to get what is desired.

Because narcissists are incapable of empathizing with others, they don't even consider (or care) how their words or actions could affect others–and they will never admit that they are wrong. Instead, they will play the victim and use the situation to gain more attention from others around them.

As with any other toxic family situation, it may be best to distance yourself from a person with NPD. This is especially true because they don't generally realize that anything is wrong. Plus, there is currently no known "cure" for NPD–though if a person affected with it seeks therapy, change is possible. However, it's very unusual for a person with NPD to seek therapy since they don't see a problem with their behavior.

"Why would someone who thinks they're special and great come for therapy?" Bloxham says.

CHAPTER 9: GASLIGHTING – A NARCISSIST'S GO-TO MANIPULATION TACTIC

What is gaslighting? Why do toxic people and narcissists gaslight you? What does it mean and how can you stop letting gaslighting bother you? What can you do to end this manipulation altogether?

If you're involved in a toxic relationship with a narcissist (or even a person with NPD or narcissistic personality disorder), then you have probably been the victim of gaslighting at some point. Used by most narcissists, this is a pervasive and highly effective tactic meant to manipulate (someone) by psychological means into questioning their own sanity. It is a pervasive manipulation technique that toxic narcissists use to control the people around them and make them do as the narcissist wishes.

Gaslighting is often about control, but it's always about meeting some need or desire the narcissist has, not the well-being of anyone else.

There are three primary stages of gaslighting, as it applies to the psychological term.

"Narcissism falls along the axis of what psychologists call personality disorders, one of a group that includes antisocial, dependent, histrionic, avoidant and borderline personalities. But by most measures, narcissism is one of the worst, if only because the narcissists themselves are so clueless." ~Jeffrey Kluger

What is Gaslighting?

Gaslighting is an ongoing form of manipulation that causes you to doubt what you see, hear and experience; in fact, to doubt your own perception of the world around you. Often used by toxic narcissists, it's a type of brainwashing that can cause you to lose your entire sense of self. Repeatedly experiencing gaslighting will destroy your self-worth and cause you to question reality.

Where does the word Gaslighting come from?

The word gaslighting comes from Gaslight, a 1944 American film, adapted from Patrick Hamilton's 1938 play Gas Light, where a husband tries to persuade his wife to believe that she's insane by causing her to question herself and her reality.

What Does Gaslighting Look Like?

It can be hard to detect gaslighting from outside the relationship. It is insidious, oddly subtle and emotionally/psychologically debilitating to the victim. During gaslighting, the toxic person makes declarations and allegations which are typically based on deliberate untruths and intentional efforts.

If you've ever had a friend, family member or co-worker who is a narcissist or who suffers from narcissistic personality disorder (NPD), chances are you have been the victim of gaslighting, which is a manipulation technique they often employ to get what they want.

"Those who engage in gaslighting create a reaction — whether it's anger, frustration, sadness — in the person they are dealing with," writes Yashar Ali in a Huffington Post article. "Then, when that person reacts, the gaslighter makes them feel uncomfortable and insecure by behaving as if their feelings aren't rational or normal."

Gaslighters make you feel crazy because they act like your reactions to their abuse is not rational. While the signs you're being gaslighted may seem "obvious" to some people, the fact is that when you're being manipulated by a narcissist, you can't always see the proverbial forest for the trees.

So if you find yourself feeling like you might be a little crazy (part of the whole gaslighting technique)—or even if you're aware that it's happening and want to recognize it as it happens—understanding the signs can be the first step to making your life a little better.

When you're aware of the behaviors that cause your narcissist to engage in gaslighting, you can react differently and change the course of the outcome.

So what are the signs you're being gaslighted?

Top 10 Warning Signs You're Being Gaslighted

Your Fears Are Used Against You—Many narcissists are very charming, at least when they want to be. Often, they will listen to every word you have to say and file away any vulnerabilities you reveal for later use. For example, if you told a narcissist you felt insecure about your weight, he might later make discreet pokes at it, or in a romantic relationship, make comments about others who are thinner than you are—in any case, he's out to feel "better" than you.

The narcissist has an ultimate goal - to make you doubt yourself so that you become more dependent on him.

You Don't Know Your Own Mind—Some narcissists will claim to know what you (or others) are thinking—and if you deny that your mind's working the way they believe it is, they might just secretly think you're lying. They might make a face or a gesture to indicate it—or in the most extreme cases of NPD, they might actually tell you that you're lying—and even accuse you of lying to YOURSELF. Because of course, as narcissists, they can't be wrong.

You Don't Know What's Normal—If you are regularly being told that things are normal when, deep down, you know for sure they are not, you're likely the victim of gaslighting. For example, say your toxic boss asks you to blatantly lie to a client about the safety of an item. When you refuse, you might be told that ALL employees lie on behalf of their employers and that if you don't want to be a team player, maybe you should find another position.

You're "Diagnosed" With Major Issues—When a narcissist is lying or manipulating a friend, coworker or loved one, and isn't getting his way, he may turn up the intensity by questioning your sanity. You might be called paranoid, stressed out—too sensitive or even hormonal. He might even tell you that you need therapy or meds to get through it. Again, it's all about being in control.

You Doubt Your Own Beliefs and Perceptions— You're told that what you know to be true is not real. For example, if your narcissist mother tells you that your significant other is a loser and that you need to dump him, after a while, you could start to believe it and might even end up sabotaging the relationship because you begin to question your own judgment, thanks to regular conditioning during visits, phone calls and emails with her.

You Can't Remember Anything Anymore—The narcissist is infamous for selective memory; that is, he will deny that he said something that upset you if you confront him on it, or he will promise to do something and later tell you that it never happened. He might also use creative language to downplay his behavior and act as though your reaction is totally out of line.

You Lie to Keep the Peace—You aren't a liar by nature and you don't lie to other people in your life. But due to the extreme stress caused by upsetting or angering the narcissist, you might find yourself at least bending the truth a little in order to avoid the verbal/physical abuse that is sure to follow any discussion or situation that is against the narcissist's "rules."

You Stop Trying to Be Heard—As humans, we are programmed to share our experiences and thoughts with the people in our lives. But when you're dealing with a narcissist and there are signs you're being gaslighted, you eventually might just give up. You stop talking about yourself around the narcissist, and depending on the depth of your relationship with him or her; you might even stop talking about yourself altogether. Then one day, when someone asks you a question about yourself, you're stumped. You might even forget HOW to talk about you.

You Start Thinking Maybe You Really Are the Crazy One—The intensity of a narcissist's manipulation tactics can really get to a person. And when you are looking for a solution (AKA a way to just END the disagreement or argument), you might just convince yourself that the narcissist is right—that there are things you could be doing better. And maybe you start to think that maybe his behavior WAS a logical reaction to your mistakes. Maybe you are the one who owes HIM an apology. And when you apologize, he eventually (probably) accepts your apology, only to later throw your "bad behavior" back in your face when it serves him.

You Are Depressed—As a narcissist wears down his victim, she may become depressed and anxious. She will constantly question herself and feel generally hopeless. If you're in this situation, you might feel exhausted from the roller-coaster ride your narcissist has been taking you on—and you might even think you're just a little oversensitive (thanks to the NPD manipulation tactics you're being subjected to.) You get confused and start to feel disoriented. And thanks to all those references to your paranoia and memory issues, you're likely to seek help for depression rather than the actual problem—the gaslighting narcissist in your life.

Even the so-called normal relationships in our lives can suffer from misunderstandings and miscommunications, but when someone starts using the manipulation tactics involved in gaslighting, chances are they might also be a narcissist—and if you're going to maintain a sense of self, you've got to start making some changes in your life.

Next, let's look at the layers and stages of the narcissist's gaslighting process.

Gaslighting Stage One: Disbelief

"The process of gaslighting happens in stages – although the stages are not always linear and do overlap at times, they reflect very different emotional and psychological states of mind," writes psychoanalyst Robin Stern in Psychology Today. "The first stage is disbelief: when the first sign of gaslighting occurs. You think of the gaslighting interaction as a strange behavior or an anomalous moment. During this first stage, things happen between you and your partner – or your boss, friend, family member – that seem odd to you."

So, in layman's terms–that means you'll find yourself wondering what just happened. You'll think the person just "sort of snapped" and that the behavior might be out of character.

You'll be shocked at some of the things the narcissist says to you - and you'll find yourself going "huh?" when he or she reacts or responds to you. A gaslighter almost seems to go out of their way to make you wonder – and that's all part of this tactic – to make you doubt your own reality.

Gaslighting Stage Two: Defense

"In the second stage, defense, the gaslightee has begun to second-guess himself," writes TheWeek.com's Shannon Firth.

This means that you start to wonder if maybe the narcissist is right–maybe you are the one to blame. You find yourself being constantly criticized by the narcissist and you being to think that you are really as slow, stupid, bad, lazy or whatever other rudeness is being spewed your way.

Again, often the narcissist doesn't even see what they're doing here–but you won't miss it. You'll feel almost exhausted by the constant barrage of insults and digs being thrown your way, and you might even vow to make personal changes in order to become whatever it is the narcissist says you're not. You lose a bit of yourself, really.

Gaslighting Stage Three: Depression

"By the time you get to this stage you are experiencing a noticeable lack of joy, and you hardly recognize yourself anymore. Some of your behavior feels truly alien," according to Marriage Advocates. "You feel more cut off from friends – in fact, you don't talk to people about your relationship very much – none of them like your guy. People may express concern about how you are and how you are feeling – they treat you like you really do have a problem."

At this point, you're probably in need of a serious life overhaul. Whether you get professional help or you simply take your power back by recognizing the serious nature of the situation and taking appropriate action to make it change–you've got to do something.

Staying in a gaslighting situation is clearly dangerous for you as a person, but in some cases, it can become even more serious since some narcissists will abuse their victims physically too.

What happens inside of a narcissistic gaslighting attack

The attacks start when you least expect them, and no matter how long you're together, they'll always surprise you just a little. They're triggered by the smallest things.

You ask the wrong question, or you answer the phone with a brisk tone that he interprets as anger or annoyance toward them.

Maybe you just look at them the wrong way at the right time. Or maybe you prove them wrong. Or you see through their lies and have the nerve to call them out.

In any case, they become a narcissist, injured. They begin manipulating you and people around you, acting like they're the victim.

They tell you and everyone who will listen how they try and try, and you're just unreasonable. They say they're the one being abused, even. There are no limits to the levels to which they will stoop to get what they want.

And that is exactly why they then use your own words against you – the ones you expressed the last time you tried to defend yourself when they attacked you.

For example, if you told the narcissist that you feel like they don't care about you because of the way they spoke to you during your last confrontation, they may use the same words to claim narcissistic injury during this one.

The narcissist repeats those words, almost verbatim, spitting them at you, projecting their own qualities on you – and making you wonder: are they right? Am I really the one at fault?

You are initially shocked to see how blatantly they twist the truth – and this shocked feeling may well continue each time these incidents occur, despite repeated similar incidents over the years.

And even when you're an old hand at detecting the bullshit, you'll still fall for it every now and then, if you're not careful.

You will try to explain the truth again. That's about the time they'll begin to devalue you and question your sanity, and if they're really skilled, you will soon begin to wonder if they're right.

If you're new to this kind of manipulation, or if you haven't yet identified it as gaslighting, the fight will start to end here, because the narcissist will realize that the manipulation has worked and that you are falling hook, line and sinker for it.

But if you know what and who you're dealing with, and you stand your ground, they may pull out all the stops.

They become a narcissist enraged, and this may alternate with the narcissistic injury.

They will dig through their mental inventory about this time, looking for the hot – button issues. You know, the ones that make you feel really raw and hurt on the inside? That sometimes cause you to lose the ability to stay focused on anything else?

Yep. Those - they will bring them out whenever it suits them, and they won't be nice about it.

If you had a bad relationship with your mother, they'll say you're acting just like her. If you recently lost your job, they will point to your failure and compare it to this situation somehow. And it'll get worse if they're aware of any kind of mental, physical or sexual abuse you've experienced in the past.

It doesn't matter what the real issue is – they won't ever address it.

Instead, they will find little things to focus on, picks on tiny little made up issues that make you the bad person to their "innocent victim." Gaslighting begins and the fight never ends – until you end it.

Your Own Personal Bully

"Bullies want to abuse you. Instead of allowing that, you can use them as your personal motivators. Power up and let the bully eat your dust." ~Nick Vujicic

Do you deal with regular episodes of your significant other raging against you, expressing extreme anger, frustration, or outrage — and have a significant amount seemingly unnecessary drama in your relationship?

Being in relationship with a narcissist is like snuggling up to your personal bully.

How do you feel after spending time with this person? Do you feel happy, relaxed, loved? Or do you feel stressed, angry, fearful or sick? Be honest with yourself. It's just you and me here.

If you're dealing with a narcissist, chances are that spending time with him or her is very bad for you in several ways. Episodes of gaslighting (and other kinds of narcissistic manipulation are used against you. As always, a narcissist's goal is often to not only mess with your confidence but ultimately to gain control over you.

Often, these episodes involve narcissistic rages in which it can feel like the world will end. These can result in hours, days, weeks or even months of verbal and emotional abuse for even the smallest incident.

When these attacks happen, your whole world will feel like it just stops, and you won't be able to function until it's over. Even then, your ability to feel normal may be gone for a long time.

What Happens Inside the Mind of a Narcissistic Supply After a Gaslighting Attack

As you sit in the cold, numb aftermath of yet another attack on your personal character, your thoughts are dulled and foggy. You can't seem to form a complete thought as the sharp, cutting insults replay over and over again in your head.

This torturous soundtrack is accompanied by a small voice in the back of your head, the part of you that remains indignant about the abuse, the part that still knows it's not normal and that you deserve better.

That part of you quietly counters the insults, reminds you that they're all a part of the manipulation tactics the narcissist uses to gain control.

That's the same part of you that truly knows that you're not in a "healthy" relationship and that there's little chance you'll successfully change this person.

That part of your mind races, struggling to form a plan to fix things, to make your escape or to at least find "normal" again. And it's that part that will ultimately help you to not just exist and survive, but also to really thrive and become the fully realized person you deserve to be.

The longer you remain in a toxic relationship, the more you deny your truths in order to avoid the wrath of this narcissist, the quieter this voice becomes.

When you deny your feelings, when you allow yourself to be told that you're not a real person and that you don't matter – you begin to act as if that is true.

And, by the basic law of attraction, you draw more of that "I don't matter" energy to yourself.

That's because you begin to vibrate that sense of "I'm not good enough." And you become inferior because you believe that you're inferior.

You feel me?

You've got to listen to that voice, or you may lose the ability to hear it. But don't just listen. Take action and do what you need to do until your life feels good.

Can you remember how it felt to have a life that made you feel good? Can you imagine a life that is good?

If you have a few minutes, imagine what would happen if you woke up tomorrow morning and found that a miracle had happened overnight and all of your problems are gone. What do you see? What does your ideal life look like?

When you can begin to imagine what you consider your perfect life, you can begin to claim it for yourself.

Trust Your Intuition

When something doesn't feel right in your gut, trust that feeling and act accordingly. That's your intuition kicking in and it's almost always to your benefit to listen and act accordingly.

Do you hide your relationship problems from people in your life? Would anyone be shocked if they knew what you were really dealing with behind closed doors?

If you are embarrassed to share details about your relationship with friends, there is a reason. Examine it and ask yourself why.

When we stop listening to our true selves, we start losing our identities. We become a shell of ourselves and begin to conform to the expectations of people who, if we're being honest with ourselves, really don't love anyone, not even themselves.

Why do we continue to allow ourselves to be abused?

As a narcissist's supply, we conform to his expectations to the best of our ability, which of course is never quite good enough. We do this, in part, because it is our nature to want to keep the peace and also to please others.

In case you weren't aware, narcissists are almost always attracted to empaths, because we are especially aware of others' emotions and naturally concern ourselves with them.

Narcissists are drawn to empaths because they are easily triggered into action by the emotions and emotional outbreaks that are so common. While some people would recoil and be repulsed initially by their behavior, empaths are wired to want to help emotionally struggling people.

And so, we spend our lives trying to fill an unfillable hole, to reach an unreachable standard.

But what we fail to realize is that it doesn't matter how hard we try – the narcissist will never be satisfied, at least not for long.

We convince ourselves that we just need to do a little better, try a little harder – change a little more, and everything will be okay.

We see ourselves becoming a "not good enough" version of someone else's ideals, rather than a beautiful, vibrant and fully realized version of ourselves.

And if we keep this up for long, our true selves are left for dead, quietly whispering our truths in the back of our minds as we desperately seek to quiet them, to shut them up and out.

All of this, so that we don't have to risk the pain of the emotions that we will inevitably face when we fully realize (and admit to ourselves) the disservice we are doing to ourselves by allowing this abuse to continue.

So, what do you do now? Once you've admitted the problem, you've taken the first step toward resolving it. Personal change must start within. We already know that there's no changing someone else – it's not your place or your right. So, you start with yourself.

CHAPTER 10: DEALING WITH OVERBEARING NARCISSISTS IN YOUR LIFE

"Our ultimate freedom is the right and power to decide how anybody or anything outside ourselves will affect us." ~Stephen Covey

So, you're minding your own business and having a bright, bright sunshiny day. Everything seems to be going your way–your kids are getting along, the guy at Starbucks finally gets your order right and the lights are all green.

Then, it happens.

Some yahoo (or narcissist) comes along and takes a crap in your Cheerios. Suddenly, your sunny outlook is replaced by the storm clouds of negativity. You start remembering all those little things that bother you, the stresses, the annoyances, and the general malaise sets in. The kids start fighting, the coffee gets cold before you can drink it and the lights turn red. You're irritated and ready to scream.

"Mean people really do suck. There you are, minding your own business, having a great day, and some snarky cashier, office person, or even a bus driver shreds your happy little bubble of a life into a million pieces," says Anne Loyd in the Mean People That Suck blog. "All you can remember is that one jerk who ruined your day."

Loyd is totally on-point. Dealing with negative people in your life totally sucks.

Most everyone has experienced this whole mean people phenomenon at one time or another, and when the negativity is doled out by a random someone in the world, it's easy to learn to change your mind and change your perspective–after all, you don't need to deal with these people on a consistent basis. Why should you let them steal your sunshine?

But sometimes, it's not some random bus driver or grocery store clerk who causes the icky feelings–it's someone you love – maybe a narcissist in the form of a stressed-out spouse, a controlling parent, or a fair-weather friend, for example. Then it becomes a whole different thing - because it feels like you can't just walk away and never see or talk to that person again. He or she is a part of your life, probably a pretty important part.

So, what do you do? Are you doomed to walking around with a proverbial rain cloud over your head? What's the trick to dealing with negative narcissistic people in your life–especially when you love them–all while keeping the sun shining in your world?

Understand What's Happening

As children, we crave the approval of the people we love. We want our parents to be proud of us, we want our teachers to think we're smart and we want our friends to think we're cool. As we grow older, we often tend to accept what our loved ones think as fact, and we internalize their thoughts and judgments against us. We begin to think that maybe they're right, that we're not good enough or that we really aren't as cool or smart as we thought.

But here's the thing that we forget. Our loved ones are human, just like we are, and in some cases, they're just plain wrong.

"Just because someone is concerned for your welfare does not mean that their advice or input has value," says writer Peter Murphy. "For example, I know a lot about peak performance. I do not know much about car maintenance. If I ever offer you advice on rebuilding a car engine run as fast as you can! My input would have little or no value."

Same deal with your loved ones–sometimes they may be negative about you or your choices because they can't understand or simply don't know how to think positively about the situation. And their lack of understanding can lead to unreasonable anxiety about your life–which, of course, makes them feel justified in throwing down some negativity on your (otherwise happy) ass. You have to learn to distinguish between valuable advice and unreasonable negativity.

Approve of Yourself

By nature, we seek the approval of the people we love. In many cases, we can feel limited and stifled by the constraints that maintaining such approval can impose on us. Some people in our lives offer conditional love, which means that they can't (or won't) treat you with love or respect unless you can be the person they want you to be.

When we don't fit into the neat little boxes that our loved ones (and our society) have set out for us, we are often ostracized or shunned, sometimes by those closest to us. And, if we require the approval of those we love to be happy, we set ourselves up for conditional self-acceptance–so when we're doing what "they" think we should, we think we're allowed to feel good about ourselves (even if that nagging feeling in the pit of our stomachs is telling us that we're not on the right path.) We become the victims of the limiting beliefs of the people around us.

We must learn to let go of the need to please the people we love and start focusing on what's right for ourselves. We must claim our independence from negativity and judgment, following our hearts to find true peace. Be yourself, and proudly claim your place in this world.

When you are happy and at peace with yourself, you'll attract more happiness and peace into your world.

Change Your Mind, Change Your Life

I've said it till I'm blue in the face: you get back what you put out into the world. So, when you focus on the negativity in your life, the bad stuff, you'll attract more of it to yourself. When you maintain a mostly positive attitude, you draw more of the same into your life.

We must own our confidence and trust in ourselves and our intuition. Keep your eye on the prize, and always expect the best–because the fact is, you get what you expect. Learn to let go of the past and focus on the positive things you've got coming toward you today.

If you've been hurt by someone you love, you must forgive that person in order to heal and move forward in peace. At all costs, try to avoid internalizing the negativity of others, and focus instead on the wonderful things in your life. We can't control the people around us, no matter how hard we try. Practice accepting yourself and the people you love for who they are and stay focused on what really matters. Be true to yourself and stay on the path that you know is right for you. Understand negativity for what it and find the approval you seek within yourself, for when you manage to achieve this new level of understanding, the rest will fall into place.

What Causes Narcissistic Injury?

Any threat (real or imagined) to the narcissist's grandiose self-perception – or the false self – as perfect, all-powerful, all-knowing, and entitled to special treatment and recognition, regardless of their actual accomplishments (or lack thereof).

In other words, the narcissist is always seeking attention, compliments, admiration and power over others in order to fill their endless need for narcissistic supply and boost their tiny little ego. This means that they could always be rejected, ignored or feel criticized.

So, in a way, it causes the narcissist to be surprisingly dependent on the compliance of the people in their life in order to feel "normal," and without this kind of narcissistic supply, they feel like they might implode.

And while the narcissist hates to admit any sort of dependence on others, they equally hate themselves for having it – and in fact, desperately fear the possibility of losing their supply – to which they're addicted like a drug.

This is a weird conundrum for the narcissist: they need people to love, admire and respect them, but they also tend to dump their emotional garbage on these same people – usually, those closest to them.

This could explain why the narcissist has a rage problem and why they seem to be secretly consumed by overwhelming envy of some people, and why they tend to attack and devalue the people they claim to care about.

Why Does the Narcissist Take Everything So Personally?

Because the narcissist is always watching for anything that could be perceived as an insult or slight, any type of criticism (even constructive) can be seen as a personal attack. The narcissist will feel humiliated and rejected, which leads to a strange kind of all-consuming paranoia. In the worst cases, this can even cause them to create made-up rules and crazy ideas, which they expect their "circle of narcissistic supply," or the people closest to them, to follow and agree with – without question.

Their defensive reactions and extreme emotions cause the people close to them a great deal of emotional pain. The narcissist isn't concerned with this and in fact, is oddly detached – perhaps to avoid narcissistic injury.

The first line of defense, of course, is to emotionally beat down (or devalue) anyone who has the nerve to criticize (or who the narcissist perceives might criticize them). This could also apply to someone who makes a joke or comment that the narcissist thinks is somehow "against them."

The narcissist will look down their nose at anyone who dares to make them feel less than amazing – anyone who dares to peek behind the mask of the false self. With blatant contempt and a rising feeling of superiority, the narcissist feels better about themselves and minimizes the feeling of inferiority. This leads to cognitive dissonance and literally causes the narcissist to lie to themselves.

CHAPTER 11: UNDERSTANDING NARCISSISTIC RAGE AND NARCISSISTIC INJURY

"Half the harm that is done in this world is due to people who want to feel important. They don't mean to do harm, but the harm [that they cause] does not interest them. Or they do not see it, or they justify it because they are absorbed in the endless struggle to think well of themselves." ~ T. S. Eliot

If you've ever been involved with a narcissist, you may be aware that when they don't get what they want, they tend to display blatant narcissistic rage, and if that doesn't work, they will jump right into narcissistic injury (or, vice versa).

What is Narcissistic Rage?

The term "narcissistic rage" was first introduced in a 1972 book called *The Analysis of Self.*

While narcissists might seem to be the most put-together people we know, calm, poised and good at managing their stress levels, anyone they feel comfortable around knows that it's all an act.

Though it would seem like narcissistic rage is always a reaction to narcissistic injury, the truth is that narcissists see it as something that is inevitable, something that was "done to them" by the person who disagreed with or was critical of (or joking about) them. This leads us to logically assume they are as illogical, unfair and outright mean – especially during the rages.

Normal anger is different than narcissistic rage. Everybody gets angry. It's normal and human. But healthier people will either work through it and use it to propel them forward into positive change, while narcissists will stew in it and let it infect anyone who has the nerve to get close enough.

Feeling threatened is just one way the narcissist will get angry. They'll also react with rage to real or perceived injustice against them, to feeling uncomfortable or being inconvenienced and to any sort of disagreement. To be fair, when we are angry, it can be hard for anyone to think and act logically, and this doesn't exclude the narcissist or their rage.

This certainly inflates the lack of empathy that is a hallmark for a toxic narcissist. Some psychologists will tell you that narcissistic rage is just something that happens and that the narcissist is actually angry at themselves, but anyone who has ever been the subject of this rage will know better.

This kind of rage manifests when a narcissist vents their frustration when their ego takes a hit. Since narcissists have an inflated level of self-importance, they often find it hard to deal with criticism, real or perceived.

So, if you or someone else happens to insult the narc's fragile ego, you can expect a serious backlash – and it's not going to be pretty.

If you're currently in a toxic relationship involving a narcissist, it's important that you understand these narcissistic rages and why they happen – and even if you've already left your narcissist, it might help you to understand WHY you were treated the way you were – because truly, it wasn't (and ISN'T) your fault.

How Does Narcissistic Rage Manifest?

The narcissist may express rage through blatant, explosive verbal or even physical attacks, using psychological abuse to minimize and invalidate anyone in their path. Or, they may go passive aggressive – using sneaky, pervasive techniques like the silent treatment to control their circle of supply. To those in its path, narcissistic rage is scary and angst-causing. It feels like nothing you can say, do, think or feel could possibly be right in the moment, and even though some narcissists will issue a weak apology later, it's clearly perfunctory and means nothing – because they'll ALWAYS do it again when it suits them.

When the preferred emotional dumpster (aka closest source of narcissistic supply) is unavailable, the narcissist will rage against random people they consider unimportant – customer service representatives on the phone, waitresses, the check-out lady at Walmart.

Narcissistic rage and narcissistic injury go hand in hand. While they often claim that their raging behavior is related to stress, the opposite is true. In fact, a narcissistic rage is triggered usually by some perceived insult, criticism or disagreement that results in a narcissistic injury.

The average raging narcissist thinks that her victim intentionally caused this so-called "injury" and that the victim did so with a hostile motive.

The reaction to this trigger is often intensely disproportionate to the actual "offense" committed by the victim—and invariably, the victim in these situations sees the narcissist as unreasonable, out-of-control, mean or even just plain old crazy.

If you're the regular target of narcissistic rage, you need to know that it is REALLY not your fault! The rage isn't about you, and it never was—it's always been about the narcissist.

Surviving Narcissistic Rage and Narcissistic Injury: Diffusing a Raging Narcissist

When you find yourself the victim of this kind of rage, you have to respond logically, not emotionally. "This is the catch-22," writes Sam Vaknin, Ph.D. "To try to communicate emotions to a narcissist is like discussing atheism with a religious fundamentalist. They employ a myriad of defense mechanisms to cope with their repressed emotions: projective identification, splitting, projection, intellectualization, rationalization."

Now, when I say respond logically, I don't mean that you should try to use logic or reason to help the narcissist calm down—this almost never works. In fact, during a narcissistic rage, there really isn't room for your opinion or side of the story at all—in fact, offering it will just prolong the confrontation.

Remember: it's not about you - it's about the narcissist. Try not to take it personally (even though the narcissist will stop at nothing to hurt your feelings and cause you to react - be prepared).

Stay Calm and Avoid Reacting Emotionally

You've got to stay calm and if possible, simply remove yourself from the situation. If you can't do that, take a deep breath be prepared to bite your tongue. Don't bother to argue or try to reason with the narcissist. Instead, just let him know that you hear their concerns and avoid raising your voice or introducing any emotion into the conversation. Respond calmly and with only facts – not emotions.

This is called the gray rock method.

Communicating with a narcissist can be incredibly frustrating, especially when it matters that they comprehend what you're saying. I can't tell you how many times I've felt exasperated when trying to have simple conversations with narcs who have become agitated and who are actively gaslighting.

They will be thicker than concrete walls, intentionally trying to misunderstand you and assume the worst of you, in every single word. You find yourself feeling hopeless, like you're unable to make your point – and if you're like me, it's especially frustrating because you probably have no problem communicating with literally everyone else in your life.

I mean – honestly, this has happened to me more times than I can count during conversations with narcissists – and I am a writer who communicates for a living.

Who invented the "Gray Rock" Method?

As far as I can tell in my research, the "Gray Rock" method was so named by a person named Skylar in 2012 at 180rule.com.

In part, Skylar says the gray rock method is, "primarily a way of encouraging a narcissist, psychopath, stalker or other emotionally unbalanced person, to lose interest in you."

How does the Gray Rock Method differ from the No-Contact rule?

Skylar says that the difference is "you don't blatantly try to avoid contact with the disordered individual."

Instead, she advises, "you allow contact but only give boring, monotonous responses so that the mentally-unwell person must go elsewhere to get their need for drama gratified."

Skylar adds: "One might say that Gray Rock is a way of breaking up with a psychopath by using the old, 'It's not you, it's me' excuse, except that you act it out instead of saying it and the psychopath comes to that conclusion on his own."

Why does the Gray Rock Method work?

According to Skylar: "There are gray rocks and pebbles everywhere you go, but you never notice them. None of them attract your attention. You don't remember any specific rock you saw today because they blend with the scenery. That is the type of boring that you want to channel when you are dealing with a psychopath. Your boring persona will camouflage you and the psychopath won't even notice you were there. This method strikes at the heart of the psychopath's motivation: to avoid boredom."

What are the most important components of successfully using the Gray Rock Method?

Rule number one when it comes to practicing the Gray Rock Method is to never tell the narcissist you're doing so. If you do, he'll definitely figure out a way to use it against you.

Never ask questions of the narcissist and don't offer any "committal" responses – just say things like "hmm" or "mhmm" – keep it casual.

If possible, discuss only "safe" topics, such as the news, social media – fashion, cooking, etc. Nothing that would be personal – even if the narc begs you for it. Drama free is the way to be!

Try to be distracted during the conversation so that you don't have to directly look the narcissist in the eye the whole time. Make it something simple like doodling in a notebook or checking your text messages, or something more complicated such as knitting a scarf or working on a document for work. If you focus a bit more on your activity, you won't be as directly affected by the narcissist's attempts to manipulate you during the conversation.

Most importantly during this practice, keep your head in the game and don't allow the narcissist to get inside your head. Narcs are expert "guilt-trippers" and have no qualms about making you "feel bad" so that you'll try to justify or defend your intentions – don't fall into the trap.

What else should I consider before I try the Gray Rock Method?

One important thing to know about the Gray Rock Method is that there is a level at which it can become unsafe for you psychologically – and that's when you begin to experience symptoms of dissociation.

A lot of people don't realize that these two are connected, but here's what happens.

When you learn to use this method and you find out how effective it can be when it comes to dealing with your narcissist, you may find that it is a great way to deal with EVERYTHING that is an issue in your life.

The problem with this is that you begin to truly stop caring – and your ability to feel your own emotions diminishes. This is a major issue because you don't just stop feeling pain and anxiety – you stop feeling the good stuff too.

Know the Narcissist's Patterns

First, understand that not a single thing you say will change the narcissist's feelings during the rage. It doesn't matter if she's arguing that the sky should be red instead of blue—she's right as far as she's concerned, and there's nothing that you or anyone else could say to change her mind. Remember: it's about controlling the situation and being perceived by you as perfect. Any evidence that she's losing control or not being perceived as perfect will further incite the rage. In order to end a rage, a narcissist needs to feel safe and in control of the situation—so if you simply want to end the temporary situation, then you may need to say whatever she needs to hear to feel that way again—especially if your safety is at stake, but even if it's just your emotional well-being you're trying to protect.

Understanding Narcissism: The Narcissist in Public

An interesting thing about most narcissists—being the charming and outgoing people they are, they project a public image of being "fun" and "laid-back," but in private, it's a whole other story. Behind closed doors, a narcissist feels safe to release his rage. And since he's so often the life of the party, the nice guy and the charmer that everyone loves to hang out with (in public, anyway), many people won't have any idea what kind of person they're really dealing with. So, unless someone personally witnesses this narcissistic rage, they can't understand what life is like for the victim/target of the narcissistic rage—especially when it's a lover, parent or family member.

Understanding Narcissism: The Narcissist and Projection

As the victim of a narcissistic rage, you've likely been accused of being selfish or of ignoring the narcissist's emotional or physical needs, of being dishonest, arrogant, lazy or any number of other insulting descriptives. But what's really happening most of the time is projection—narcissists project their own inadequacies onto their victims. So as usual, it's all about the narcissist, not about you.

The Narcissist and Selective Memory

Narcissists are infamous for their selective memories. They may claim they said something that they never really did—and then get angry at you for "not listening." Or they might even deny saying something that you KNOW they did say, but now regret. And, they're likely to contradict themselves in the same breath, lashing out at anyone who points it out to them. In either case, you might feel like you're going a little crazy when this happens—and it's a sign of gaslighting.

The Narcissist and You

When you love a narcissist, you have to understand your role in her life. A narcissist really doesn't have any interest in being emotionally or intellectually stimulated by the people in her life. In fact, feedback of any kind can be perceived as a threat. People who love narcissists have really clear roles in their lives: they are the primary source of "narcissistic supply;" that is, they are expected to supply the narcissist with the admiration, respect, love and attention the narcissists believe they deserve. But when these "suppliers" fail in their mission (in the narcissist's opinion), the rage often turns against them. "A passive witness to the narcissist's past accomplishments, a dispenser of accumulated Narcissistic Supply, a punching bag for his rages, a co-dependent, a possession (though not prized but taken for granted) and nothing much more," Vaknin writes. "This is the ungrateful, FULL TIME, draining job of being the narcissist's significant other."

Understanding Narcissistic Rage: What Causes a Narcissist to Rage

Psychologists have identified several typical causes for narcissistic behavior and personalities, including a general obsession with self, often gained through certain experiences during childhood. They often have an addiction to anger, and as they rage, it's often because of a blow to their inflated sense of self-esteem.

They may often make self-deprecating statements, no doubt silently begging you to disagree with them and tell them how amazing, beautiful, wonderful and perfect they REALLY are...and when you don't, the rage could begin.

Like I said, a narcissistic rage often launches when narcs become defensive because they think you're insulting them (or if you attempted to communicate a problem or concern about your relationship with one).

They may also be caused when a narcissist finds himself feeling unfulfilled and blames the victim/target for that feeling.

He feels powerful when he rages, and he isn't likely to stop until his requirements are met.

As we've previously discussed, narcissists believe that by appearing perfect, they can get the love, admiration, attention and/or respect they feel they deserve. But when they think that someone feels they're "not perfect" or "not good enough," they often find themselves feeling shameful or anxious. Sometimes this can manifest as guilt or anger.

In any case, when a narcissist's self-esteem takes a hit, he might react in a number of ways on a broad spectrum—anywhere from just being mildly irritated all the way to having seriously explosive tantrums that can even become violent in some cases.

This kind of "narcissistic injury" causes the narcissist to need to destroy the perceived threat to his self-esteem, and by raging against the offender/victim, the narcissist is able to feel safe and powerful again—and like he or she has total control over the environment.

Understanding Narcissistic Rage: Different Types of Rage

There are three primary types of narcissistic rage, including explosive rage, passive-aggressive rage and rage that causes self-harm.

An explosive rage happens when a narcissist has a violent outburst, whether it's physical or verbal, while a passive-aggressive rage is expressed when a narcissist passively punishes the victim. He might do this by ignoring the victim, by being blatantly rude or even by doing nice things for another person and flaunting them in her face.

In any case, you'll know it's happening, and he'll feel perfectly fine with telling you you're crazy and pretending he's not doing anything at all.

In some cases, he might even be so bold as to inform you of your infraction and require you to submit to the punishment willingly in order to make your way back into his good graces.

When a narcissist manifests his rage through self-harm, you might not understand what's happening. It doesn't seem consistent with his personality —but it DOES get him plenty of attention. Some narcissists have been known to cut, burn or even stab themselves, among other extreme self-injuries, during a narcissistic rage.

CHAPTER 12: BEING A NARCISSISTIC SUPPLY

"Narcissists are people who never learned to make it on their own. Except for their fantasies of perfection, envy of others who have what they lack, and unacknowledged fears of humiliation, they are empty on the inside. They have no real Self to bring to a relationship with another person, but they desperately need someone else to join them in their emptiness and help them maintain emotional equilibrium. The ideal candidate is someone willing to become an extension of the Narcissist's fragile ego, to serve as an object of admiration, contempt, or often enough both. The sign over their door ought to read: Abandon Self All Ye Who Enter Here." ~Sandy Hotchkiss, Author of Why Is It Always About You?

Narcissistic supply is anything (or anyone) that a narcissist sees as supportive of their overblown self-image. This can be either a direct or an indirect affirmation. Usually a person but can also be a pet or group of people, the narcissistic supply is used by the narcissist to get attention, validation, admiration – all the "supply" they need to feed their ego. The narcissist often has a circle of supply or "narcissistic harem."

In layman's terms, a narcissist needs attention in the same way that you need air. They need love, admiration and in general, one-way narcissistic supply. This supply often comes in the form of a narcissistic harem, AKA a circle of supply.

What's interesting is the various roles we play when we are a source of narcissistic supply. If we're part of the narcissistic harem, the roles might include such roles as:

The Tool – This special member of the harem has an important role. She's there to not only "get" the narcissist in her own clutches, but also to cause drama for the rest of the members. She lives on a pedestal built by the narcissist and they often claim they "just haven't met the right person yet."

The narc considers this person a challenge because she, like he, is unlikely to commit, so she seems hard to get.

Flying Monkeys – In the case of the narcissistic harem, the flying monkeys often mean well, but they end up evangelizing the narc's message without even realizing it. Flying monkeys are often just other causalities of the narc's manipulation tactics, but they're always falling for it.

The Old Standby – This can be an ex or a person who is just generally "there" for the narc when he needs attention. Generally ends up causing drama, especially when the Tool finds out about her.

The Wife/GF/Husband/Spouse – Depending on the narc, there's almost always a partner – a "main" person in the harem. While the partner isn't always a legal spouse or even the one who gets the most attention in the narcissist's harem, she's the one they're all hiding the secrets from – and maybe the worst role you can be stuck with.

Between the gaslighting, love bombing and flying monkeys, you end up forgetting your own identity as you desperately try to become the version of yourself that would make the narcissist happy.

But even if you manage to completely change yourself and morph into the narcissist's idea of the imagined perfect person, it never matters.

Painful Truth: You Will Never Be Enough for a Narcissist

Here's a harsh reality that we all have to understand. When it comes to the narcissist and his perception of you, you can never be enough. Even if you completely focus your energy on a narcissist, he or she will always look for somewhere else, something else to increase their own "supply" of attention. No matter how amazing you are – it will never be enough for a narcissist.

Don't let yourself be confused here – it's DEFINITELY not YOU! It's totally the way the narcissist's convoluted mind works, and you can't take personal responsibility for the broken person you're dealing with – you just have to find your way to self-confidence and peace OUTSIDE of the narcissist.

The fact is that since the narcissist is so personally "broken" on the inside, nobody on earth can ever fill the endless hole of "need" he carries around – at least not for long.

There are so many manipulation tactics that most narcissists have in common that most of their victims say reading about the abuse suffered by others can feel like reading their own stories. Their tactics are underhanded and sneaky – often undetectable. And yet, they're so definable that even a child can learn to recognize them.

Why is narcissistic supply so necessary for a narcissist? Because without it they are likely to go into self-destruction mode, which can serve a number of purposes – most importantly, of course, the generation of "alternative supply sources," because without these sources, the narcissist will crumble and even become psychotic in some cases.

Consider the case of Gus Fring from *Breaking Bad*, and AMC's *Better Call Saul*. While he's more likely on the psychopathic end of the cluster B spectrum, he's someone you'd never suspect when you first meet him – he works as the fair-minded, soft-spoken owner of a small chain of successful chicken restaurants who is unfailingly polite and doesn't seem like he could hurt a fly. But when you see him kill someone with zero regret in his face and clean himself up without one ounce of apparent nervousness, you realize what you're seeing. He's always totally in control – except when he isn't. His narcissistic rage presents itself in the form of murder and torture – extreme forms to be sure, but a legitimate depiction of the psychosis that can affect a person with NPD.

CHAPTER 13: THE IDEAL SOURCE OF NARCISSISTIC SUPPLY (WHAT NARCISSISTS WANT)

"Understanding how a narcissist works is the key to living or working with one. If you can understand his or her behavior, you may be able to accept it as you realize their behavior is NOT a result of anything you did or said despite them emphatically blaming you. If you can accept their behavior and not take the abuse and other actions personally, you can then emotionally distance yourself from the narcissist. If you can emotionally distance yourself, you can either cope with the narcissist or garner the strength to leave." ~ Alexander Burgemeester, The Narcissistic Life

The beginning of a relationship with a narcissist can be very deceptive; in most cases, a narcissistic relationship begins just like any other—with the standard phases of initial attraction, infatuation and eventually falling in love.

What type of person does a narcissist go for?

There is no single "type" that a narcissist typically goes for, technically—there are no parallels to be drawn among the partners of narcissists as far as height, weight, eye color, race or any other physical or cultural characteristic.

While there seems to be no "ideal" or "standard" mate/friend/spouse for a narcissist, there are certain similarities about the relationships. For example, the narcissist typically begins a new relationship with a "honeymoon" period, during which everything seems perfect, almost too good to be true.

Living in a relationship with a narcissist can be anything from exciting and exhilarating to soul-sucking and traumatic. And it usually is one or the other depending on what day it happens to be. You might compare it to a type of emotional rollercoaster.

And a narcissist cannot exist without someone to adore them, submit to their will, be available at their whim and willing to disparage themselves to the narcissist's benefit. Their whole identity really depends on it—it's called narcissistic supply. So, what draws a person into this type of relationship and keeps her there?

Common Qualities Among the Partners of Narcissists

"The inherently dysfunctional 'codependency dance' requires two opposite but distinctly balanced partners: the pleaser/fixer (codependent) and the taker/controller (narcissist/addict," writes Ross Rosenberg. "Codependents — who are giving, sacrificing, and consumed with the needs and desires of others — do not know how to emotionally disconnect or avoid romantic relationships with individuals who are narcissistic — individuals who are selfish, self-centered, controlling, and harmful to them. Codependents habitually find themselves on a "dance floor" attracted to partners who are a perfect counter-match to their uniquely passive, submissive and acquiescent dance style."

While physically, culturally and otherwise, the victims of narcissism aren't the same, there are certain qualities that typically unite them. I'm going to use the "she" pronoun here but note that there is no single sex that is a typical victim.

First, she must be insecure or at least have a distorted sense of reality, if you expect her to stick around. Otherwise, she'll be out on the first or second exhibit of narcissism, early on in the relationship.

She will likely often belittle and demean herself, while glorifying the narcissist and putting him on an untouchable pedestal.

As a result, the partner becomes the victim, which works fine for her—she tends to punish herself. Maybe she's even a bit of a masochist. She probably feels like she "deserves" this life of torment.

She's his eternal scapegoat, always put-upon and putting her own needs last.

"It is through self-denial that the partner survives," says Sam Vaknin, a self-proclaimed narcissist. "She denies her wishes, hopes, dreams, aspirations, sexual, psychological and material needs, choices, preferences, values, and much else besides. She perceives her needs as threatening because they might engender the wrath of the narcissist's God-like supreme figure."

Victims of narcissism often call themselves "people-pleasers" or "diplomats," but the truth is, they are often so downtrodden in relationships that they just become changed, reactive versions of their former selves.

"When you are the partner of a narcissist, you are there to project the image he wants for you—that he wants his partner to project," writes Diane England, PhD. "Of course, your house and lifestyle probably fall into this category, too. They are all about making statements to others he wishes to impress, not about providing you with the type of environment you might find comfortable or restful–an environment that feeds your soul."

Have you ever noticed how, if you've found yourself in one toxic relationship with a narcissist, you often find yourself in another (or more) at some point in your life?

Why does this happen? Have you ever asked yourself questions like these?

- Why do I keep getting into relationships with narcissists?
- What is it about me that makes me attractive to a narcissist, anyway?
- Or what about narcissists that attracts me every time?

I know I have. Can you relate? Why do we keep finding ourselves in these kinds of relationships and what can we do to avoid this in the future?

Three Reasons You Might Be an Ideal Source of 'Narc Bait'

I have a few theories. Let's start here.

You're an Empath or HSP

One of them is that those of us who tend to attract narcissists tend to be empaths and other "HSPs"- highly sensitive people – who are wired to sense and react to the emotions of others. To a narcissist, an empath can be like crack – it's that whole "vampire/fairy" factor from the HBO show True Blood.

You're Trying to Fix Your Broken Childhood

Another theory is that we're working on fixing our own "issues" from childhood or earlier in our lives.

"We choose our partners because they represent the unfinished business from our childhood. They manifest the qualities we wish we had. In doing so,

choosing such a challenging partner, and working to give them what they need, we chart a course for our own growth."

I heard this quote in an episode of Modern Family that I happened to catch a few weeks ago and it really stuck in my head – it really made me think – isn't it possible that one reason we find ourselves attracting narcissists is because, each time we deal with one, we never really HEAL afterward? And subconsciously, we're trying to solve the unfinished business from our childhoods? I think yes.

You Avoid Confrontation Like the Plague

A narcissist has a way of testing people early on in the relationship, and if you are one who will be willing to "work through anything," or you get upset but ultimately let them have their way, a narcissist knows he's struck gold. So if you're the sort of person who tends to be a "people pleaser," or to be often described as "too nice," watch out – you're exactly what a narc looks for in a person.

CHAPTER 14: DETOXIFY YOURSELF AND YOUR LIFE

If you're dealing with a narcissist or otherwise toxic family member or friend, you've probably got a lot of someone else's thoughts floating around in your head.

You might think you're not good enough. You might think that your feelings and thoughts aren't genuine or relevant to the world, and you might even feel like a big fake when you do try to follow your dreams, simply because you've heard for so long that you're not worthy, whether directly or indirectly.

If you're struggling with a toxic relationship, especially a family-based one, you may have had so much conditioning that you aren't even sure which way is up.

The first step to healing is to start within your own head. You have to change those thoughts and limiting beliefs that are holding you back.

Fix yourself first. Then you can make the choices you need to make to remedy the situation and make your life better.

When I was in my own toxic family situation, I struggled with feelings of hopelessness, worthlessness and more. I felt like nothing I did or said was genuine or worth knowing about, like I had to hide who I was in order to conform to the expectations of my toxic family member.

But I learned some important lessons as I began the healing process, and I want to share them with you. If you're currently in this situation, you may have never heard these things - and when you first read them, you probably won't even believe them. But these are truths - and I want you to keep reading them until you get it.

Changing your mind will help you to change your life. I'm living proof it works.

Remember:

Do not let a narcissist ruin your self-worth. Know that you are good enough.

You are a real person with legitimate concerns, thoughts, feelings and aspirations.

You are good enough.

You don't need anyone's approval or endorsement to help you succeed. You can get validation through success in your own, self-dictated endeavors.

It isn't about you and that it isn't your fault. You aren't bad or broken.

You can literally do almost anything you want to do if you simply decide to do so. If you choose to do it, you'll be compelled to take inspired action and you will make it happen.

You have something real to offer the world. You matter. You have value.

You can be exactly what you choose to be and choosing your own identity does not make you selfish, lazy, entitled or otherwise unsavory.

You define YOU. Never a narcissist to tell you who you are.

You get to choose your own identity every day. You decide who you are and how far you go.

You can compromise for someone you love to a certain point when it's time to choose your priorities and choose a path. But compromise means that both parties bend and both parties are satisfied with the outcome. It's not compromising to give up what you truly want in order to make someone else happy or to keep them from getting angry at you.

If you were to walk away from the toxic relationship, the world would not end. But it will be very difficult, and you'll have a lot of soul-searching to do. Personally, I had to reexamine everything I understood to be true.

Detoxify Your Thoughts

"Being in a good frame of mind helps keep one in the picture of health."
~Unknown

You know all about toxic families and toxic friends, but have you ever considered that your own thoughts can become toxic?

This is especially true if you love a narcissist–and even more especially if you live with the narcissist.

We've talked before about why it's important to keep an eye on your thoughts–because you bring about what you think about. So, if you're focused on all good things, then more good things will come your way. But, if your thoughts become toxic, they can and will draw negativity and toxicity into your life and can even cause physical side effects if left unchecked.

Research has proven that the way we think can cause a wide variety of chemical reactions in our bodies. When we're thinking happy thoughts–forgiving people, feeling patient and maintaining self-control, for example–our bodies will release chemicals that make us feel peaceful and healthy.

But when we're feeling negatively and thinking toxic thoughts–like feeling and nurturing rage, holding grudges or wallowing in guilt or self-pity–our bodies release damaging chemicals. This makes us more susceptible to illness and disease.

Narcissistic rage can further complicate the situation, especially because narcissists typically aren't aware that they have the ability to BE wrong–and if they are, forget about it–you're going to have a cranky person dealing with a severe narcissistic injury.

Dr. Caroline Leaf, author of the book *Who Switched Off My Brain*, says that "stress and anxiety harm the body in a multitude of ways; patchy memory, severe mental health issues, immune system problems, heart problems and digestive problems."

Serious stuff, right? The way you think can literally affect not just your day-to-day quality of life, but also your long-term health.

So how do you stop thinking toxic thoughts?

Listen to Yourself Talk

You may not even realize how often you complain or lament about the things in life you don't love. Maybe you are frustrated because you had to wait in line for a half hour at the grocery store, or the traffic on your way home from work was so terrible that you actually got out of your car and sat on the hood to get a little sun. Perhaps you found out that your kid failed Science or you didn't get into the college of your choice–or your dog ate your knitting project.

If you're a narcissist, you're probably not reading this anyway - but those of us who are dealing with you are likely to get the brunt of your toxic thoughts. So hey, if you love us, why not try to get a brighter perspective? We'll love you for it.

And honestly, does it really help you to rehash and focus on these negative things? Nope, it actually hurts you. So, while you should absolutely feel comfortable telling the people you care about what happened to you during the day, try to focus on the positive side of things, even when there doesn't seem to be one.

For example, if you waited in line at the grocery store, maybe you talked to someone who really needed a good conversation. If you sat in traffic too long–maybe you needed the solitude, or you heard your favorite song. You get the idea–find the silver lining in every cloud.

How to Stop Toxic Thoughts: Use Mind Control (On Yourself)

I can't stress enough how important it is to recognize and monitor your thoughts. You may not even realize how often you think negative thoughts. For example, if your friend wins an award that you wanted, you may think "she must be better than me" or "I deserved that award, not her!" But if you can bring yourself to genuinely congratulate and feel happy for your friend, you'll not only do her a favor, but yourself too.

If you find yourself FEELING negatively, take a minute to listen to your thoughts. You might be surprised to find out that you may be subconsciously thinking toxic thoughts.

Take control of your mind, because you can. All you need to do is mentally cancel those toxic thoughts and replace them with positive and healthy thoughts that reflect your true desires. (Because whatever you think about and focus on is what you're drawing toward yourself–so why not think about and focus on what you really want?)

Change Your Scene

When I feel like my thoughts are getting a little toxic, sometimes it helps me to just change the scene around me. Maybe that means just going into a different room or taking a walk–or maybe I need to get in the car and go somewhere. But inevitably, if I make the effort to change my scene, it changes my mind pretty quickly.

Try going out for coffee with a friend, taking a walk or a bath, working out–
or even busting out the Wii for a little karaoke or golf. Whatever works for
you–just get away from the spot in which you started thinking toxic thoughts
for awhile.

CHAPTER 15: WHERE YOU GO FROM HERE (LIMITS, SCHIMITS)

"Don't limit yourself. Many people limit themselves to what they think they can do. You can go as far as your mind lets you. What you believe, remember, you can achieve." ~Mary Kay Ash

As you are probably painfully aware, a really great life doesn't happen by chance. It's the result of your intention, and of having goals and skillfully allocating your resources in order to reach them. These resources include your thoughts, time, and energy.

Ultimately, a great life comes from taking the time you're given each day and using it with intention. This is more effective than just dealing with the next item on your endless list of chores or reacting to what's happening around you.

The key is in being proactive to create the life you desire.

Anyone who knows me probably knows that I do everything within my power to stay positive about every situation. And it serves me quite well. Still, occasionally something sticks in my head and I just have to talk about it.

Like, for example, the fact that every year, I read a ton of Facebook posts people make about New Year's resolutions – many of which often say something to the effect of "be sure to set goals, but don't shoot too high."

I'm here to tell you that is complete nonsense.

Stop whatever you're doing for a minute and read this:

The fact is that you won't get more than you expect.

Hold on. Read it again. Really GET what I'm saying before you keep going.

You ONLY get what you expect.

So, let's say you'd really like to open your own business. Now, you could resolve to do that, and if you believe that it will manifest (and take inspired action as necessary), the world is your oyster.

But, let's just say you're one of those Negative Nelly or Ned types and you don't believe it can happen.

You worry about not having enough money, not having enough support, not being able to get the loan or the employees or WHATEVER it is that you are afraid of – and then, my friend, you might as well just pack up the idea before you even get started.

Why? Because you get what you BELIEVE you will get. If you believe you will have "not enough" then expect it. You've got to focus on having "more than you need" or everything you need IN ABUNDANCE if you expect to get anywhere.

Fact: You simply cannot achieve more than you believe you can.

It's not that complicated, really. Like Mary Kay Ash once said, "If you think you can, you can. And if you think you can't, you're right."

Read carefully my friend: Do Not Put Limits on Your Desires! You can have, do or be whatever you want, if you believe that you can. You don't have to know exactly how you're going to get there, either.

That's one of the cool things about this whole deal–put your desires out to the universe and then believe that you're manifesting them. Because you are.

You are what you think. Placing limits on your thoughts (or attempting to limit the aspirations of others) will only attract more limits into your life. Instead, open your mind and recognize that the world is abundant. You can achieve whatever you believe you can.

Think I'm full of it? Think of Andrew Carnegie. The child of poor immigrants, he believed that he could achieve his dreams–and went on to become the second richest man in history. So how did he do it? He simply believed that he could–he decided what he wanted, took the necessary inspired action, and his true divine desires manifested exactly as he expected.

"I am no longer cursed by poverty because I took possession of my own mind, and that mind has yielded me every material thing I want, and much more than I need," Carnegie once said. "But this power of mind is a universal one, available to the humblest person as it is to the greatest."

In case I haven't made myself clear, don't believe anyone who tells you that you need to put limits on your goals and desires. You are the keeper of your own destiny, and YOU decide what you believe you can accomplish. Refuse to accept anything less than your true divine desires.

Still not convinced? Remember what Buddha said: "All that we are is the result of what we have thought."

Think big, my friend. Believe that your greatest desires will manifest— because the truth is that we really do get what we expect.

Need a further nudge? Consider what famed American writer and mythologist Joseph Campbell said.

"Follow your bliss, and doors will open for you that you never knew existed. Follow your bliss, and the universe will open doors for you where there were only walls."

A Life-Altering Exercise

I know, that last part was pretty intense. But it's truly possible. Just in case you're struggling with figuring out exactly what you want the next part of your life to look like, I've created this simple but life-altering exercise for you to try and help you figure it out.

Take a moment for yourself.

Sit back, relax and allow yourself to dream for a bit about whom you'd like to be and what you'd really like to do with your life. If you could simply paint an image of who you want to be, what would that look like? Free-association like this can be incredibly helpful in realizing your goals.

Spend some highly productive time meditating on your dreams with these strategies:

Find a quiet time and place.

This will be somewhere where you can reflect without interruption. You might take a walk in the park or a bike ride for an hour. Maybe you'll choose to lay out on a blanket under that big shade tree in your back yard.

Encourage your mind to pursue any positive thoughts.

Think about what you wanted to be when you were 10, 15, and 20. Was it the same occupation or way of life at each stage of your development? Or were you always coming up with something new you wanted to do?

Think about your deepest desires.

Do you want to have a lot of money and travel the world? Or just settle down and have a family? Perhaps you picture yourself surrounded by many close friends with whom you spend a lot of your spare time. Maybe your preferred way to live is an independent, quiet lifestyle alone with your books, paints, and hobbies.

Visualize your living space. Where you live largely determines the kind of life you have.

Living in a warm southern climate means you can be more physically active in warm weather year-round. If you live in an apartment in the middle of the big city, you might live a life filled with wall to wall people, ethnic foods, and cultural experiences of all kinds. There's rarely any quiet and you're incredibly active, partaking of all that city life has to offer.

A rural setting, on the other hand, provides its own sense of stability. You enjoy nature frequently. The sights, sounds, and smells of plants, animals, and the four seasons surround you as you walk or work outdoors. Stress levels are lower.

Make a wish.

You might think that making a wish is just for kids. But for the sake of this exercise, if you could have just one wish for your life, what would it be? To be a husband someday? To be a mother? To travel to a few exotic countries you've wanted to see? To be an accountant or small business owner?

Your wish will reveal a lot about you and what you desire.

Dream about your career.

Continuing to paint the picture of who you would choose to be, where would you be working? What kind of job credentials would you hold? What would you be like in that situation?

Because work is almost one-third of your life, consider your career choice as profoundly integral to your happiness.

Do a little planning.

Now that you've reflected on your life and who you'd like to be, how close is your actual life to your desires? What can you do to help yourself become who and what you want to be?

You deserve to live the life you choose.

Reflect on who and what you want to be. Let your mind go for a bit. Then, ask yourself what you want for yourself. Think about where you'd prefer to live. Think about the career you'd have if you could do it all over again.

Finally, ask yourself what you will need to do to get to the place of your dreams, physically, emotionally, and career-wise. You can be anything you want to be. Make some effort now to find out who that really is.

Do you know who you are? And what are you going to do about it?

CHAPTER 16: FORGIVE, DON'T FORGET (THE LETTER)

When I was in college, I rented a basement from a friend and her boyfriend. Rent was cheap and we could carpool to both school and work.

Things went great until their relationship began to deteriorate, at which time my friend moved out.

We all agreed that I would continue to rent the basement, at least until they decided what to do with the house.

In the few weeks I lived there after my friend moved out, her boyfriend began to go into my things while I was gone, taking things and doing who knows what else.

He made it no secret either–on several occasions he confronted me about various items or information he found among my private belongings.

And then, one day, I woke up and found that he'd climbed into my bed while I slept. That was the last straw. He had violated my privacy and now he was violating my personal right to choose who was allowed in my bed.

Since I couldn't wait until I found an apartment to move out, I crashed on a friend's couch for a few days while I located a new place.

When I finally did, I was very happy–except for the overwhelming anger that kept looming in my subconscious. Every time I turned around, something reminded me that he had hurt me, violated me, upset me. And that he wasn't the only one who, by the time I was 19 years old, had done so–some in even more harsh ways.

Negativity begot negativity, and I started seeing more and more of it in my life. I struggled with it for months, falling into depression after depression. I felt like I was completely worthless, drowning in my own thoughts.

One day, as I sat wracking my brain about how to get over this anger, I thought I heard something. I was alone in my apartment, with the exception of my cat. And I know this is going to sound crazy, but I would swear to you that I heard someone whisper, "You have to forgive him," in my ear.

And, more strangely, I knew immediately what the "whisper" meant.

Even though I'd stuffed it all down and tried not to focus on my anger for all of these months, it still stayed there, like a parasite, nibbling away at anything positive that came into my life.

So, I picked up my notebook and started writing him a letter. I told him why I was so angry at him and what he did that hurt me so much. I told him why I thought he was wrong. I called him every name in the book and said cuss words that I invented for the occasion.

And at the end of the letter, I told him that I forgave him–not for him, but for myself. Because I deserved to live in peace, without the negativity of my past with him (or anyone else, for that matter) corroding my beautiful world.

When I finished the letter, I felt an amazing sense of peace come over me, almost immediately. And, while I'd fully intended to mail the letter (or at least an edited and polished version of it) to that man, I never did. It turned out that I didn't need to.

Once I'd written down my feelings, owned them, and moved on–the healing began. Such a simple act allowed me to release months of pent up feelings that were holding me back. I was finally able to begin to feel GOOD again, and suddenly my life was back on the right track.

How about you?

Are you holding a grudge? Do you have some old anger lingering in your heart? If so, it's time to begin to heal. We all know logically that we cannot change the past, so why live there?

Here's my challenge for you today. If you are plagued by anger or holding a grudge that you just can't shake, try writing a letter today to the source of your frustration. Say what you mean, and don't censor yourself. Let it all out.

And then, offer your forgiveness.

Then, if you like, write a more "reader friendly" version of your letter and mail it to the person or people who have hurt you. But more likely, you might find that the simple act of getting it all out is enough, like I did.

The bottom line here is that if you are holding on to toxic anger, it's only hurting YOU. The person or people you're angry at are probably not aware of it–and if they are, it's not affecting them nearly as significantly as it is you.

The best revenge, they say, is living well–so if you don't want to let go of your anger just for your own sake, then let it go to be the bigger person.

I'll leave you with a final quote from Catherine Ponder.

"When you hold resentment toward another, you are bound to that person or condition by an emotional link that is stronger than steel. Forgiveness is the only way to dissolve that link and get free."

CHAPTER 17: THE OPINIONS THAT MATTER, AND THE ONES THAT DON'T

"It took me a long time not to judge myself through someone else's eyes.
~Sally Field

How many times have you not followed your heart because you were worried about what other people might think? How often have you avoided doing something you truly wanted to do because you couldn't stand the idea that other people would judge you?

Have you based your major life choices on your own desires, or have you allowed other people to influence you? Do you have regrets because you have given someone else the power to make decisions in your life, whether directly or indirectly? Have you chosen your job, a partner or your home because someone else thought you should?

You're Not Alone

Most everyone has, at one time or another, made a choice in their lives that was based on someone else's opinion. And while there are certainly times when it's appropriate to do so, there are plenty of times that we regret not following our own intuition.

The difference is this: when you accept the advice of someone else because you feel that it's right for you, you're following your own gut and can consider it inspired action–but when you bend to someone else's will to please them (despite your own feelings), you're shortchanging yourself in the happiness department.

Why Do We Care What Other People Think, Anyway?

It's human nature to care what other people think. From infancy, we learn that when we do what someone else wants us to do, they're happy with us–and that feels good. As we get older and learn to make the occasional unpopular decision, we are sometimes shocked to learn that some people actually seem to stop being nice to us when we don't follow their "advice" for living.

But ultimately, we care what people think because we are taught to base our identities on the messages they give us. When our parents tell us we're good for following their rules, for example, we begin to feel that we need to follow the rules to be good. When our kindergarten teachers scold us for coloring outside the lines, we begin to feel that unless we "stay inside the lines," we're wrong.

We take the messages that we hear from others about ourselves every day of our lives, and we internalize them–to such an extent that we find ourselves dependent on the approval of others for our own self-worth.

Should We Just Stop Caring?

Of course, this is a two-sided coin. While we certainly need to learn to follow our hearts and our own intuition toward inspired action and to make our own life choices, there are times we need to follow the rules. For example, to be productive members of society, we need to follow certain societal norms–at the very least, we have to follow the laws of the land.

And, the fact of the matter is, most of us aren't able to just "turn off" caring about what others, especially those we care about, think about us and our choices. We don't want to become cold and immune to the emotions of others, but we want to be happy. To be happy, we must make our own choices, follow our own divine inspiration for what we want our lives to be. At the end of the day, we're the ones who must live with the decisions we make.

So, where does this leave us? Are we doomed to an eternal internal struggle? How do we start taking charge of our own lives and stop letting the judgments and opinions of others dictate our choices?

So often, we're so afraid of what might happen if we don't bend to the will of others that we never feel safe in making our own choices. What will they think of us? What will they say? Will they think we've all turned into huge jerks?!?

Kate's Story

Thirty-seven-year-old Kate, for example, says that her father has always dictated her life choices. He pressured her to attend his alma mater and to follow in his footsteps in her choice of career. He bought her a home next door to his own for her college graduation gift, got her a job at his firm, and steered her toward a specific man when he thought it was time for her to get married. He has essentially made (or manipulated her into making) every major life decision for her–and she is angry.

Let's put this in perspective, shall we?

Kate, a 37-year-old woman who is capable of taking care of herself financially and physically, feels that if she doesn't do what her father thinks she should, she will be abandoned by him, physically and emotionally. Kate admits that she fears that her father won't love her anymore if she doesn't do what he says is right–and that deep down, she believes that she is obligated to play by his rules because she would be Alone In the World without his support.

Do you recognize Kate?

Kate seems to have a problem that many people have–she's a people pleaser. She has learned to base her own self-acceptance on the acceptance of other people in her life. Jay Earley, Phd says that being a people pleaser is a learned behavior, usually starting early in childhood.

"Often, parents will simply tell kids what to do and never encourage them to assert themselves," Earley says. "When the kids obey, the parents give them conditional love."

Time to Make a Choice

Here's the bottom line–if you want to be happy, you must look inside of yourself to find out what you truly desire. And then, you must go after it–regardless of who it's going to piss off.

Easier said than done, I know…but what's the alternative? Living a life that's been designed and approved by someone other than you. Pick your poison, folks.

Be happy and follow your heart or do whatever someone else says you should do–and deal with the consequences. If you choose to be happy and to make your own choices, I applaud you (not that you need my approval or anyone else's)–and here are a few tips to help you get started.

Get Some Perspective

Honestly, what is the worst thing that will happen if you make a choice that someone else disagrees with? In most cases, there may be a brief period of discomfort in the relationship with that person before he or she accepts your decision. Of course, there are some people who would actually cut you out of their lives for such an infraction–but those are the people who love or like you only conditionally. ("If you do what I think you should, then I'll love you" kind of people.)

Do you really want people like that having so much control in your life? Evaluate the relationship. Is it toxic?

Believe What You're Saying (and Doing)

One of the biggest reasons people feel comfortable in telling you what to do with your life is that you accept (and expect) that they will. That causes you to doubt your own inner voice–you know, the one that tells you what you need to be happy.

Next time you make an unpopular choice in your life, do so with confidence, and when or if you choose to share your decision with someone who criticizes it, be prepared to smile and say something like, "I understand and appreciate your concern, but I've thought this through and have chosen ______________ carefully." And then leave it at that.

When you acknowledge and are grateful for the fact that the person cares enough to tell you his or her opinion, he or she might feel validated and accept your choice a little more gracefully. Remember: you're not asking for permission or approval. You're stating a fact–this is a choice that you have made. End of discussion.

Take a Cue from Earl

If you've ever seen the TV show called *My Name is Earl*, then you'll know what I mean. At first glance, Earl looks like a former convict who lives in a cheap motel and shares a bed with his brother. But if you take a second look, you'll notice something special about him. He observes the people and situations around him, but he never judges or belittles them. He doesn't react negatively–he just observes.

Remember that like attracts like–so if you focus on judging or disapproving of people and situations in your own life, you're likely to find that people judge or disapprove of you and your situation. Focus instead on accepting other people around you, and you'll find yourself more accepted by others.

Accept Yourself

Speaking of accepting people, how about extending the same courtesy to yourself? If you're secretly judging and disapproving of your own choices, you need to figure out why. Is it because you're doing something that you believe is wrong? If so, you need to reevaluate your motivations and figure out why.

Is it because someone else thinks what you're doing is wrong, even though you're happy doing that? If so, it's time to stand up and be who you are–and to be happy about it. People who love you will be happy that you're happy.

Remember that you don't need to hold the whole world on your shoulders!

I don't know about you, but sometimes, I find the idea of asking for help can leave a bad taste in my mouth - no matter how much I need it. Our society teaches us that we should be super-human–able to hold down a full-time job (or two), raise a family, maintain a marriage, friendships and more–all while looking positively fabulous.

We're always looking for new ways to save time, do more, be more–always trying to improve, find ways to just BE MORE than we are. But here's the thing. There are only so many hours in each day, and you've gotta spend a few of them sleeping. It's a fact.

Another fact: a single person cannot possibly know everything, cannot possibly excel in every area–and most importantly, a single person cannot hold the world on his or her shoulders. Read closely: It's okay to ask for help. Repeat it to yourself: it's okay to ask for help.

CHAPTER 18: INSECURITY AND THE HARD TIMES

"Narcissistic love is riding on the rollercoaster of disaster filled with a heart full of tears." ~Sheree Griffin

Insecurity sucks. And for a narcissist, it's a secret that most people aren't even aware Of – but while the narcissist has the ability to appear completely together, in reality, he's a big ball of insecurity and self-hate.

What you may not know is that it's also a narcissist's goal to make you feel bad about yourself.

Why would that be the case? It's all part of how their brains work – and it's part of the gaslighting and manipulation so many narcissists inflict on the people they're involved in relationship with.

You might feel like you're all alone when you're dealing with a narcissist in a toxic relationship, but the truth is that getting involved with one of these "Jekyll and Hyde types" is something a lot of people go through at one time or another. Sometimes, though, people have to endure so much soul-numbing mental abuse from their partners, which can have a powerfully and profoundly negative effect on them that lasts a lifetime.

After a painful episode of gaslighting or other forms of narcissistic abuse, it's sometimes very difficult to bounce back from the mental abuse you had to endure and your self-esteem plummets because of it.

Not only that; the torturous mental abuse you were subjected to by a narcissist is usually an attack on your personal character – an emotional assault committed all too often by the narcissist.

The narcissist needs to make you feel worthless and insecure, but you don't understand why – you'd be their biggest fan they'd let you.

Why does a narcissist want to make you feel worthless and desperate?

It's basic NPD 101 – the narcissist's intent (whether he realizes this or not) is to gain control and boost his or her own ego (yes, women can be abusive, too).

Bottom line? The narc wants you to have low self-esteem, so you won't think for yourself. In an ideal situation, this is the time to go "no contact" (NC). The truth is that getting out of a toxic relationship like that is the first step you need to take in order to save your own sanity. But sometimes, NC isn't possible. What do you do then?

You learn how to deal with it. Here are some tips to help.

How to Get Through the Tough Times with a Narcissist

There are other things you'll need to do to recover fully from the gaslighting, manipulation and mental abuse that you are experiencing (or have experienced). It's important to stay active.

Start by getting "back to your life" – so get out and do things with your family and friends, because an abuser loves to alienate you from your loved ones.

Keep your mind focused on other things so that you don't isolate yourself at home and become dependent on the negative person who's feeding into your self-esteem issues. I have found that focusing on what I CAN control (as opposed to things that are beyond my control) is especially helpful – you have to change your mind to change your life, right?

Call your friends, read uplifting books or concentrate on a project like redecorating your house.

Do whatever it takes to keep you going. If you have a job, continue to work and take note of your goals and achievements. If you don't have a job, look for one. Working can get your mind off of your problems and give you the necessary affirmation that you can do whatever you put your mind to – and that you're not worthless.

Don't waste time obsessing over the narcissist – whether it's negative or otherwise. Some people make the mistake of spending a lot of time with thoughts of how much they hate their former partner or how they wish they could get revenge.

Release the anger and focus on what's important – you! It's time to move forward with your life. Don't be afraid to seek some professional help. A coach or therapist can help you work through your feelings and help you

build your self-esteem back up. Don't let a toxic relationship break your spirit
– get out there and take back your life!

CHAPTER 19: WHY IT'S SO HARD TO WALK AWAY FROM A NARCISSIST

"If it's so bad, why don't you just leave?"

Have you heard this question one time too many? My guess is that if you said yes, you probably also know what it feels like to walk on proverbial eggshells all the time. You might be in a toxic relationship.

Toxic Narcissism: Pretty on the Outside

When you're in a relationship with a narcissist or sociopath, it often looks nearly perfect from the outside, especially to people who aren't aware of the dynamics that happen behind closed doors.

And most likely, you don't want anyone to know how ugly your relationship really is on the inside. Am I right?

If you're in a toxic relationship with a narcissist, and you still manage to talk to someone outside of the relationship about the problems you have, you've probably heard the "why don't you just leave" line (or some version of it) more times than you care to admit.

But what the (probably genuinely) concerned friends and family members don't know is how very, very complicated your life can be.

The Complicated, Convoluted Price of Loving a Narcissist

When you love a narcissist, you might be mentally exhausted already – and for anyone else to add problems to your plate? The sheer thought of it makes you want to vomit.

You might find yourself becoming increasingly isolated in an attempt to maintain your sanity. The simple act of engaging with normal, happy people can make you want to run and hide, sometimes.

And in some cases, your narcissist will do everything in his power to add to your isolation, to make you feel more alone – and to put you in the position to be completely dependent on him, physically, emotionally and even financially.

What They Don't Know Can Hurt You

While you understand that your friends and family members love you and mean well when they ask you questions like this, it can seriously affect the way you see yourself and your life.

Often, you forget that you're even "good enough."

In fact, for many people in relationships with narcissists, it gets even more serious. Not only does your self-esteem take a nosedive (as if there were much lower it could go at this point), but the isolation factor brings trouble to your relationships with other people in your life.

Why Friends and Family Cut You Off When You Won't Leave

Often, a concerned loved one becomes tired of hearing about your problems and cuts you off because they can't stand to see you go through that – they don't understand "why you just don't leave if it's so bad."

You have no choice but to let them walk away, because you're so exhausted already and you don't even have the energy to explain to them anymore. Then, of course, your abuser gets what he wants – you, more isolated and under his or her control.

And you? You feel more trapped than ever.

Why You Hate It So Much When They Ask Why You Stay

It's probably one of the most upsetting and annoying questions anyone could ask you, when you're in the thick of a narcissistic relationship. So, why does it bother you so much when someone asks you why you don't just leave?

For one, you're the only one who really knows how very complicated that would be to make your escape.

Plus, you know he or she will make it as difficult for you as possible if you do choose to go. And, in many cases, you've lost a lot of friends and don't have much money of your own – the narcissist made sure of it long ago.

The Narcissist's Spider Web of Control

The more your abuser can control in your life, the more you can feel trapped in the narcissistic "web" of control.

And often, the people who love narcissists don't even see it happening. But bit by bit, they tinker away on your personal boundaries, repeatedly and systematically crossing them, one by one.

Before you know it, you're in the middle of your worst nightmare – and you can't tell anyone about it because you're so…damn…humiliated.

Because you know better, you're smarter than this – and because, honestly, you don't want anyone to see how weak you've become.

And somewhere in your mind, you focus on the good stuff, because you know that it's right around the corner. It's part of the ups and downs you experience in a narcissistic relationship.

Know This: It is NOT Normal, No Matter What the Narcissist Says

Despite the bullshit they're feeding you, the way your narcissist is behaving is NOT normal. In fact, if your relationship with a narcissist were a mental illness, it might look something like bipolar disorder – extreme highs and the lowest of the lows.

The most intense pleasure and the most profound pain. Exhilaration and exhaustion. The happiest you've ever been…and wishing yourself dead – all in the same day. You feel me?

But I'm here to tell you something an amazingly intelligent woman once told me: love isn't supposed to hurt.

Stop. Read this once more: *Love isn't supposed to hurt.*

How does that sentence make you feel? Have you come to believe that being in emotional pain is part of love? Apparently, it isn't.

And know what else? Love isn't supposed to beat you up, mentally or physically. Love should make you feel safe, not afraid, not trapped. Love should make you feel free.

Are you being emotionally abused? Know the signs.

According to the Domestic Abuse Project, the kind of emotional abuse inflicted by a narcissist is the most pervasive type of abuse – the one kind of abuse that is often overlooked even by its victim.

"Emotional abuse is harder to pin down or prove, but it's just as destructive as other, more obvious forms of violence," the foundation's website says. "We consider it domestic abuse if a person makes cruel, unfair comments or otherwise emotionally attacks their partner in order to gain power or control over that person."

According to the foundation, signs of emotional abuse might include your spouse or partner engaging in the one or more of the following activities on a regular basis:

swearing or screaming at you (part of narcissistic rage)

repeatedly harassing, interrogating or degrading you

attacking your self-esteem or insulting you, such as name-calling, put-downs, and ridicule

attacking or insulting people you care for, like your family and friends

blaming you for everything that goes wrong

forcing you to do degrading things, like making you kneel, or making you beg for money

criticizing your thoughts, feelings, opinions, beliefs, and actions

being extremely jealous

telling you that you are "sick" or "crazy" and need therapy (also known as gaslighting)

using physical disabilities against you, or putting you down for your disability

blatantly ignoring and denying basic facts and make up lies that better suit him or her (also part of the gaslighting process)

Do you feel trapped in a relationship with a narcissist? Are you being emotionally abused? Be honest with yourself. It might just change your whole life – and in a good way. Knowing there's a problem is the first step to creating a better outcome.

CHAPTER 20: THE TOXIC LOVE DRUG

"What fascinates me about addiction and obsessive behavior is that people would choose an altered state of consciousness that's toxic and ostensibly destroys most aspects of your normal life, because for a brief moment you feel okay." ~Moby

Similar to Stockholm Syndrome, trauma bonding is a condition that causes abuse victims to develop a psychological dependence on the narcissist as a survival strategy during abuse. Trauma bonding also makes recovering from a toxic relationship significantly more difficult.

Trauma bonding makes it harder for you to resist the urge to connect and reconnect with the narcissist. It makes you keep wanting to go back, over and over again.

Why and how a narcissist can suck you back in every time

What's wrong with me? Why do I keep going back to the narcissist? Why do I miss him so much when he was so terrible for me? Why won't she just leave me alone?

Believe it or not, these are some of the biggest questions I hear from both readers and coaching clients as they work through their narcissistic abuse recovery program. Almost always, when you finally gather up the nerve to end a toxic relationship, you're going to be faced with a rocky road at first.

Most narcissists will try to get your attention again after you've been separated – whether it's immediately or after a period of time. And many survivors of narcissistic abuse admit that they get sucked back in from time to time.

Speaking of "sucked in," let's remember that narcissists love to "hoover" you when they feel like they've lost control of you. Read more about hoovering here.

Oh, and let's not forget the love-bombing of it all.

What if you're the one trying to get back together with the narcissist?

Now, if you're the one trying to reconnect with the narcissist, you're probably experiencing a lot of emotional abuse right now – it's exactly the type of thing a narc enjoys. You'll repeatedly go through the devalue and discard phases, peppered with brief episodes of reprieve in which you almost catch a glimpse of the person you once knew.

If you think about it, the psychology of people who have been abused by narcissists is so altered by the abuse that their reactions to things that happen in their life aren't "normal," for lack of a better word.

What does that mean, exactly? Well, let me offer up a quick example using puppies. (Stick with me here, it's not as crazy as it sounds!)

The Happy Puppy and the Biting Puppy

Let's say that you were out to buy a puppy. You find a group of perfectly adorable pups and it's time to make the choice.

One puppy seems happy and friendly, and when you hold out your hand, he sniffs it and offers up a little doggie kiss.

Another puppy seems a bit stressed, to say the least, and when you hold out your hand, he bites your finger, drawing blood in the shape of his tiny little puppy teeth.

A "normal" response would be to take the happy puppy home and never think of the biting puppy again, while a person who has experienced narcissistic abuse is more likely to keep going back to the biter and hoping for different results. Or even to choose that one because you feel like no one else will – or because you think you can "fix" it.

The fact is that it's "normal" for us as humans to go toward pleasure and away from pain – after all, pain is a warning sign that something is WRONG. You feel me?

Along the same line, let's get back to those dogs for a moment.

Think about the stories you've heard about dogs who stay loyal to their owners who hurt them. Why would they do that?

It's because of programming – the training and conditioning that you instill into them, along with their need to look to their "pack leader" for guidance.

How is this relevant to your situation?

Well, the fact is that if you're going to voluntarily return to someone who has abused you, you've experienced a similar kind of conditioning. And sort of like the dog, or even like hostages who experience Stockholm syndrome, you find that you become addicted to the need to please the narcissist, or the need to find out if he or she is okay, or even of the need to get some of his coveted "positive" attention, if that's what he's been depriving you of – those glimpses of what he once was. This is what brings you back, at least on one level.

And, like the dog who is beaten, the narcissist uses fear to control you – and when you've gone no-contact or when you threaten to, the narcissist reaches deep into his manipulative toolbox and pulls out your biggest fear of all the fear of being utterly, desperately alone.

So, in a way, you have to recognize that the feeling of obligation and almost desperation that you feel when you're away from the abuser isn't real.

The Ugly Truth: Maybe You Keep Going Back Because You're Scared That the Narcissist Was Right

The bottom line, though is this: the reason you want that abusive person back, even though they put you through absolute hell, is because the pain of the idea of being ALONE, abandoned, helpless, worthless – that's so much worse, in your mind, than the actual abuse.

Sometimes, having someone who just seems to have all the "right" answers – someone who keeps you right on the edge of sanity – just feels like home, especially if you've been stuck in a toxic relationship for long.

And that, my friend, is where we all sort of figure out where our places are in this world – it's part of what makes us attractive to narcissists in the first place.

And what makes them attractive to US – they can sort of seem like what we've always wanted, our hero, our savior – that is, until we discover that they've been secretly consuming our souls, one bite at a time. Before you know it, you're left spinning and feeling empty.

So how do you get over the need to keep going back to the narcissist?

You've got to change your mind. I know, it sounds simple. But if you change your mind and literally DECIDE that you don't need him, you'll eventually get there – even if you have to fake it a little at first.

Use the law of attraction to your advantage by employing a simple-to-remember mantra or affirmation that you repeat to yourself anytime you have feelings or thoughts that make you want to go back.

And, if you have to, create a little "narc-resistance" file – one where you write down or record your reasons for leaving – and staying away – and make sure you're very honest with yourself – after all, no one else needs to see it.

The Toxic Addiction to the Narcissist

Logically, you know you shouldn't do things that are bad for you – like drugs. And toxic people who are bad for our lives – we all know we need to get/stay away. It's just not always so easy.

See, what people don't always realize is that we are sort of addicted to the abuse we've suffered from our narcissists – and when we don't do anything to manage our addictions, we might find ourselves falling back into our old habits, right?

It's just like when you've been a lifelong smoker and one day you quit cold turkey. You KNOW the cigarettes were killing you, but they tasted SO good and made you feel so relaxed…and because you're currently trying to quit, you feel like just one could relax you and take the edge off – and maybe you think you can handle it.

But before you know it, you're back to your 3-pack-a-week habit and your brief freedom from them is but a memory.

Same deal with the narcissist.

Something you should know: Romantic love actually stimulates the same area of the brain as addiction. So, your addiction to your narcissist is not really your fault – your body sort of goes into survival mode. Your primitive mind tells you that you NEED the narcissist.

Why?

According to scientists, we're biologically programmed to behave that way. There's an evolutionary spin here – the loss of a potential baby-making mate would be bad for us as a species. On top of that, humans are hard-wired to develop bonds to other humans – another survival urge.

Add together your biological need to bond and the need to keep your mate (or to feel great distress in the loss of him/her), and what do you have?

It affects you like a drug, your relationship with this toxic person. And when you're not getting the sweet poison, you might just miss it. A lot like a crack addict might miss his fix.

And, just as much as your body wants to protect you from losing your narcissistic love, your brain wants to lie to you about it and offers up only selective memories in times of great stress.

Let Go of the "What Ifs" If You Ever Want to Heal After Narcissistic Abuse

Anyone who has found herself alone in the world has, at one time or another, reflected back on an old love and wondered "what if?" – whether we admit it or not, am I right?

But when the "what if" is geared at a toxic and painful past relationship, sometimes your memory can be a bit selective – especially when you're feeling weak and vulnerable in your life.

For example, if you recently left your narcissist and you have managed to get a job, save up enough money for a down payment on a new home and get the paperwork going on a nice little place you can call your own, it would seem like everything should be good.

But on the other side of that coin, there's the natural trepidation that anyone experiences in the face of big life changes – and of major life purchases. That kind of feeling – of being on the precipice of personal evolutionary shifts – it can leave you feeling vulnerable, scared and in desperate need of some familiar-feeling comfort.

And it is in those moments of weakness that we pick up the phone and we make the call, or we text the message that we're desperate, and we need him, and we miss the "good" old days.

It is those moments in which we forget about all of the gaslighting, the name-calling, the painfully awkward silences that almost hurt your ears more than the screaming and excruciatingly personal insults.

These are the times when we need to remember why we left. The time when educating ourselves on narcissistic abusers can help to increase our resistance to their tactics and behaviors.

When we are armed with knowledge and understanding of the patterns and typical behaviors and motivations of narcissists, we can better resist and protect ourselves from them, and from falling for their tricks.

Managing and Overcoming the Trauma Bond

"Being trauma bonded to an abuser is being tied to something you know harms you yet still feeling unable to get away. The emotional ties alone are confusing and challenging." ~Lise Colucci

*Author's Note: The remainder of this chapter was written by my fellow QueenBeeing narcissistic abuse recovery coach, Lise Colucci

If you are experiencing trauma bonds you may notice how difficult it is to put any attention on yourself except to feel the pain of the trauma bonds. One effect trauma bonding to a narcissist has on you is that it creates an overwhelming impulse to be thinking about the narcissist or trying to rationalize what happened in the relationship.

The gripping emotional pain and the way your mind wants only to think about the narcissist or the pain they caused you can make it feel impossible to even try when a suggestion of self-care is given. There are ways to help you through this and ideas for self-care which can be done simply throughout your day.

Self-care can take many forms, the more commonly thought of things like pampering yourself or treating yourself to something nice may not work for everyone when deeply trauma bonded. It may feel artificial or be hard to enjoy when your mind is on the narcissist. When things are really at a low point you may not even have the energy to do extra pampering things and think self-care will come later, once you feel better.

One thing to remember is self-care works, it just takes repeated efforts and many types of care to get there for some of us. A big piece of breaking trauma bonds is in taking back your life. Once you begin to feel your own joys and your own excitement about life and your activities you will begin to focus more on self and less on the narcissist.

Over time, and with healthy amounts of self-care the bonds lessen, and you will feel your focus shift onto things you want to think about instead of things you have been in a sense forced to because of trauma bonds.

Here are 5 ways to use self-care in your everyday life:

Nurture yourself in everyday activities.

As you go about your day barely functioning it may seem impossible to think you can use any amount of self-care or add in anything new because of the exhaustion you feel. This is the perfect time to learn how to make self-care a lifestyle. One of the good things that can come out of being a survivor of narcissistic abuse is you can learn to care for self in a more compassionate, mindful and deeper way through your healing process.

What works great here is to look at the things you will do in a day and add some positive thought or intention to a few of those things. For instance, you are likely to shower or at least brush your teeth, instead of going about these tasks in a business-like way and letting them just be tasks, use the time to experience self-care.

As an example, try adding in positive intention before showering by thinking something like, "I will let this water wash away a layer of my pain." Before you get in set the water temperature to just the way you like it and allow yourself to feel the care you are giving to self through small gestures.

Appreciate yourself and try noticing things like the scent of the soap. Understand that you are taking the time for you. It only takes a few seconds and with practice can become a part of your daily routine. Try this when you eat, when you dress, when you take a walk (even if it's just from your house to your car). Pretty much any activity can have an ounce of self-care added to help you regain your sense of self again.

Use your senses

Using your senses for self-care can be the most nurturing thing you can do for yourself. It is especially useful when trauma bonded because it directs the attention, without words, to a more nurturing experience and reaches your emotions without the need for a lot of thinking,

The fastest way to the emotions is through the sense of smell. Since the sense of smell can trigger emotions it's important to find positive scents that please you to have around. While scent may get to the emotions the fastest, all of your senses are important for self-care.

If you can think of ways to use all of your senses to truly nurture yourself, you will be showing yourself love and care in easy to do simply ways. It's the kind of care that needs no words and is simply felt. After all the thinking you are likely doing while healing from trauma bonding it can be the perfect break from thought.

Here are a few ideas for using your senses:

- Get out in nature and experience the sights, scents, and sounds.
- Walk barefoot in the grass or soft dirt/sand
- Choose a favorite food and really let yourself taste it as you eat
- Light scented candles
- Put on your most comfy outfit
- Curl up in a cozy blanket
- Pet an animal
- Sip your favorite hot drink
- Music
- Wear your favorite color
- Get yourself flowers and put them where you can enjoy them

Find an outside focus to put your attention on

When you've trauma bonded, your mind can feel stuck on thinking about the narcissist or the pain they have caused you. You may feel almost obsessed with understanding what happened and why.

Understanding is so important, and I think for some people, critical to not only healing but to their not allowing another narcissist into their lives. Seeking understanding, however, needs breaks of focus so that you are also getting the nurturing you need in your day.

One way to get a break from the thinking about the narcissist is to find an outside focus to learn about or revisit. Maybe it's a thing you used to love and have not done in a while that you might take up again, or perhaps it's something brand new.

Taking time each day to seek out not only new things to learn or try but to revisit old things you once did and loved will help you to create a thriving self as the trauma bonds heal. It is never too soon to start this, even if you are still with the narcissist.

Self-care in this way helps us have a sense of who we are which is so quickly lost to narcissistic abuse. That sense of self, as it is restored or maybe gained for the first time will bring you a freedom that is totally separate from the trauma bond and help to allow those bonds to be less intense and eventually heal.

Allow for your feelings but add in breaks for your nervous system

The feelings you are experiencing are real and need validating but after a lot of time feeling so bad it can be extremely draining. By giving yourself breaks from the stress you will build hope for healing.

Taking a break will also calm your nervous system some and bit by bit this will add up to feeling better. I am not suggesting dissociating but rather shifting focus for a limited time to get some relaxation and relief from the trauma bonds.

Some ways to get an emotional break in healthy ways might be:

- Meditation
- Set a task to do that will take ten-15 min and do it with all of your attention
- Take a nap
- Gently tell yourself it is ok to have a break from the pain then take a walk
- Create art- paint, draw, photograph, anything that allows you to create
- Get active

There is a lot of adrenaline and cortisol coursing through you when being abused and that can cause a lot of issues for your health and body. Movement can help to begin healing that. It may feel impossible to get out and exercise and if that is the case do it right where you are.

At any moment stretch, move your arms around, do a squat or two, try a plank, or just touch your toes (or knees if bending hurts). Work within your physical limits and move!! your body care at the same time. Your body takes on a lot of stress from emotional abuse, things, like dancing or even swaying to music, may give you nurturing care. You may find that yoga, Pilates. dance or another exercise class which includes core work and stretching very beneficial. For now, if that is too much to add to your day, just move your body with love and intent on healing.

What are self-care ways that help you to get through emotional pain? Can you think of things you might do to nurture another person and then try them on yourself? What will your life look like once you are healed and thriving?

Take a few minutes and free-write in your journal on these questions.

CHAPTER 21: CONSIDERING NO CONTACT

"No Contact doesn't mean No Contact except for x, y and z. By No Contact, I mean NO — zero, nada, zilch — Contact. To use Freshmen Orientation parlance: No means no." ~Shrink4Men.com

So, you're considering going "no contact" with your narcissist. Congrats, you're on your way to finally taking back your life. Are you ready to leave? Have you already left, or are you still trying to decide what to do?

In any case, you need to know something important: it's not your fault that you feel so drawn to your abuser.

But why do you still want your narcissist when the narcissist is or was so terrible to you?

Why is it SO HARD to go no-contact?

Since you're here, reading this information, chances are that you've already figured out that you're in a relationship with a toxic narcissist, and that you at least need to consider going the "no contact" route, if you ever want to be happy again.

But, as I'm assuming you know, that's a whole lot easier said than done, especially when the person in question is a close friend, family member or significant other.

In case you're not aware of what "no-contact" means in reference to narcissistic relationships, let's start by defining it.

What is No Contact?

No contact is a technique that you can use to begin the healing process after a toxic relationship with a narcissist. It is essentially required to heal after narcissistic abuse and the trauma involved. It involves removing yourself from the narcissist's life. It isn't easy, but it is necessary if you ever want to get yourself back.

The No Contact Rule, Defined

Simply put, the "no contact" rule is enacted when you end ALL contact with toxic narcissist. This includes but isn't limited to the following.

Stop taking the narcissist's phone calls.

Block him/her on all social media networks.

Do not schedule or encourage visits with the narcissist.

Stop seeing, speaking to or in any way interacting with him/her.

It's not rocket science, right? Then why is it so difficult to enact and then to stick to the no contact rule?

Because, as I mentioned before, it affects you like a drug, your relationship with this toxic person. And when you're not getting the sweet poison, you might just miss it.

As you can see, no contact is simple. You stop seeing, speaking to and interacting with the narcissist. You block them on social media and on your phone. You do not communicate with them at all unless you're forced to because of shared children or the business of divorce.

In those cases, you use what we call "limited contact" or low contact. This means that when you DO contact them, it's only regarding the business you have to discuss. No emotion should be used or acknowledged during these communications. You use the gray rock method.

Going and staying no contact not only allows you to heal, but it also allows you to clear your life of the negative energy they bring into every room.

Get free resources to help you with going and staying no contact: visit QueenBeeing.com/No-Contact

CHAPTER 22: TAKING BACK YOUR POWER

Have you ever wondered why some people seem to have it all? I'll tell you why. It's because they believe that they can have it all, and they believe they deserve it.

Ever wondered why you can't get anything right? Well, here it is folks: it's because you don't believe you can.

The great automaker and apparent philosopher Henry Ford said, "If you think you can do a thing or think you can't do a thing, you're right."

He was exactly right. My message to you is simple. The power you seek to change your life is in your hands. All you have to do is use it.

The really cool part is that it's so easy—just believe in yourself. Stop doubting yourself and watch your thoughts. When you notice negative thoughts, just say to yourself, "I'm now canceling this negative thought and replacing it with this more positive affirmation of my true desires."

In fact, you don't even need to be that formal about it—but reciting something to that effect in your head is a great way to distract yourself from the negativity you're dealing with, and then it's important that you actually follow through and replace the thought with a positive one.

For example, let's say you are calling a creditor to explain why your payment will be late. Before you call, you might worry and tell yourself that they won't understand, and that they'll be rude or nasty to you.

When you make that call, you find that your fears come true. And here's the interesting part…it came true because you believed it would.

Next time a situation like that presents itself, visualize yourself being clearly understood and empathized with by your creditor. Visualize the situation working out to your best advantage, and really know it. Tell yourself things will work out in your favor, and really believe it.

I'll bet you have a different outcome this time. Give it a shot. You won't regret it!

Bottom line: If you can believe it, you can achieve it. It's a fact.

Here's how you avoid falling off the proverbial wagon and stay in control of yourself and your healing.

Do you ever find yourself feeling like you've completely lost control? Do you worry about everything, even the things you can't do anything to change or control?

If you're anything like I used to be, you might even find yourself feeling sick with worry sometimes. It doesn't mean you're bad or wrong – it just means you're normal and that you're not alone. Many survivors of narcissistic abuse find themselves overcome with worries, thanks in part to the abuse they've suffered.

I mean, think about it. When you're always concerned about how the toxic person in your life is going to react to everything, you develop a terrible habit of feeling stressed out all the time – and this, of course, leads to not only mental health issues such as complex post-traumatic stress disorder (C-PTSD) but also to a myriad of physical effects and health issues. If you want to stop stressing about things you can't control, stick with me here – and try the seven tips I'm sharing with you today.

Worrying is a habit that many of us believe is helpful in some way, but the fact is that that worrying only has a negative effect – and that is especially true when we're worried about things that we have no ability to affect.

Worry less and live more with these strategies:

1. Put your worries in perspective. I know how it feels to worry, believe me. And when you're dealing with a toxic person, worries can overwhelm you really quickly. But try to shift your perspective a bit here – this is something you CAN control! You are in charge of how you see yourself and how you choose to perceive the situations in your life. For example, if you're still in a relationship with a toxic narcissist, you may be worrying about how you're going to get out. Instead of focusing on the worry, focus on empowering yourself with a plan to escape and on how you're going to live your new, narcissist-free life! Or, if you're worried about something like your weight, stop focusing on worrying about it and start doing something to change your situation right away – stand up right now and do 10 jumping jacks, or maybe get online and research more effective ways to eat healthier.

2. Expect good things to happen. Going through narcissistic abuse makes you pretty pessimistic if you think about it. And who could blame you? After all, every day you spend with a narcissist feels like your own personal hell – right? But here's the thing: now that you're moving on (or preparing to), you need to stop expecting the worst and start expecting the BEST. Seriously, The fact is that you can't worry if you expect a positive outcome. When you assume things will turn out poorly, they often do. If you need to, make sure you're as prepared for the worst as you can be - but be optimistic. Your worry isn't going to change anything.

3. Understand what is and isn't under your control. We spend a lot of time worrying about things we can't change. What's the point? Do what you can to mitigate your risk and then see what happens. Let go of the things you can't control. For me, learning this stuff was a HUGE factor in creating positive personal change in my own life. The moment I gave myself permission to stop worrying about things I couldn't control; I instantly felt a sense of relief and my life seemed to be so much less painful. This intentional practice is SO powerful when you enact it!

4. Stay grounded in the present moment. It's all about being mindful. Mindfulness is another (free!) powerful tool that we can use as survivors of narcissistic abuse. For the duration of our toxic relationships, we spent so much time feeling helpless and out of control that many of us found ourselves sort of living in our own heads. But if you intentionally change that and bring yourself into the present moment, you'll find that your worries can disappear. Do this by paying attention to what you're doing right now. Avoid thinking about tomorrow if it stresses you out. Use pattern interrupts if you need to do that to stay focused. A few simple pattern interrupts include brushing your teeth, showering or any personal care act; walking or running outside; switching up your location in the house or office; standing instead of sitting; listening to good music that makes you feel happy, etc. Make the best use of your time each moment and the future will take care of itself.

5. Practice gratitude. I know that it feels like we don't have a lot to be grateful for sometimes – especially when we're still dealing with a toxic person in our lives, but those are the times when it may be most important to practice gratitude. When you realize how much you do have to be grateful for, the future isn't as scary somehow. Remind yourself of how good your life is already, even if you start with things like "I'm grateful I woke up today." You'll worry less.

Remember: Gratitude is a habit. Take a moment each day and mentally list the things that you're grateful for. This can do more to enhance your perspective than you think. I like to use my own gratitude practice as part of my intentional vibration management. Try starting your own gratitude journal.

6. Avoid isolating yourself. During and after toxic relationships, it's common for victims and survivors of abuse to isolate themselves for a number of reasons. But life is harder to manage all alone. It's not reasonable to assume you can do everything by yourself. It's also less stressful to have a few friends in your corner. Avoid isolating yourself just because you're stressed. Your stress will only increase. Stay in touch with others. If you've lost a lot of friends and family members due to the toxic people in your life, try joining an online support group for narcissistic abuse survivors to make connections with people who understand what you're going through and to get yourself moving in the right direction again. Visit QueenBeeing.com/group-support for a list of free support groups.

7. Look at the facts first. Statistically speaking, we worry about way more than we need to – or at least, more than we should. The fact is that you've probably worried about a lot of things over the course of your life, right? How many of them actually came true? And how often did you worry about things that you had no ability to control or even affect? You'll likely discover that most of your worry was inaccurate or unnecessary.

Most of the things we worry about never happen. And even if they do, it's not nearly as awful as we anticipate. Conclusion: Any time spent worrying is wasted time. If there's something you can do to resolve the situation, just fix it. Life is short and worrying detracts greatly from life. Work to minimize the amount of time you spend worrying each day. You'll enjoy life more, you'll be less stressed, and you'll be one step closer to living your very best life!

Stop Worrying Journaling Exercise

Ready to take your narcissistic abuse recovery to the next level? Grab your journal and do the following exercise. If you prefer, you can just consider the questions and meditate on them instead.

- Take a moment to think about how much time you spend worrying each day. Has any of that worrying ever accomplished anything positive in your life?
- Think about the things you worry about. Make a list of your concerns.
- Evaluate your worries. Go back to your list and decide which of your worries are under your own control – as in, are there things you can do to change the outcome of the situation you're worried about? If the answer is yes, take a minute to write down the actions you can take to change or affect the situation. If the answer is no, cross the worry off your list.
- Imagine what you could do with all of that time and energy. Imagine how much happier and comfortable you would be if you could minimize the amount of time you spend worrying each day. What would it mean for you? How would your life look if you didn't have so many worries? Take a few minutes to write down your ideas.

CHAPTER 23: THE END OF THE TOXIC RELATIONSHIP

So, you've made the choice to end your relationship with a narcissist. Or maybe the choice was made for you. I want to tell you to feel amazing about that right now. But first, let me tell you this – I know it hurts. And that's okay; it's going to get better. I promise you.

However the relationship ended, you're working on recovery from the narcissistic abuse you've been suffering.

From gaslighting to playing the victim to flying monkeys and beyond, narcissists know only one thing: they want what they want when they want it, and nothing else will do.

Research proves that narcissists, regardless of their classification and level of extremity, all share four basic traits – they lack empathy, they are self-centered, have a serious disregard for other people and they are selfish.

I polled several of my narcissism support groups and they agree that this seems consistent with their experiences. How about you?

Back to you: Starting the Healing Process

The first thing I want to tell you, whether you're already gone or you're planning your escape, is congratulations.

I know that might seem inappropriate at this moment, but try looking at it a new way.

Imagine the level of freedom you can now enjoy. Imagine how you'll be allowed to make your own decisions, to be the person that you truly want to be.

The Big Secret: Deep Down, You Really Are Who You Want to Be

See, the truth is that the person you want to be is secretly who you really are – so the best way to begin to find yourself and figure out your life after narcissistic abuse in a toxic relationship is to indulge in the things you love, the things that make your soul feel alive.

That's going to help to discover yourself and bring that "true you" up to the surface.

But what if I love to do something I'm no good at? What will that serve?

First of all, you'll never know until you try. Plus, you don't have to be "good at it" to enjoy it; but about now, I'd love it if you could stop feeling like you're not good enough.

You being "not good enough" is simply a lie you've come to believe thanks to the mind-numbing experience of being involved with a narcissist.

A toxic relationship with a narcissist can literally kill you

It's a narcissist's nature to tear down the people who are closest to him or her. The narcissist must feel in control, and they must obtain what he considers the appropriate amount of admiration and attention from their various sources of narcissistic supply.

When they get it, he feels validated and he might be the best guy you've ever met – or she might be the coolest girl.

Note: Narcissists come in all shapes, sizes, colors and sexes.

But when the narcissist finds himself spending too much time alone or with a lack of attention and admiration, or he's directly defied, he becomes a whole other person.

When Narcissistic Rage and Narcissistic Injury Set In

Narcissistic rage and narcissistic injury will set in and the person in the line of fire is most likely to get the brunt of the narcissist's rage.

In fact, narcissists know very well how to manipulate you; often they'll play the victim in order to get you on their side (narcissistic injury).

When you fall for it, they might just inadvertently recruit you to become one of their toxic flying monkeys. Or, if you don't, you can probably expect the injury to become rage. And then if you don't finally comply with serving his needs, the narcissist will likely send a flying monkey your way to do his manipulative bidding.

When you feel weak: How to stay strong in the face of a love bomber

We all know that when a narcissist feels like he's lost (or might lose) something he wants (yes, I said something, because to a narcissist, people are things), he goes into love bombing mode.

You know, that's when he places you on a pedestal and makes you feel like you're perfect and amazing and like no one can compare? And where he suddenly seems humble and sweet and you start thinking maybe he really can change, after all? And then before you know it, he's back in and you're back to trying to figure out how to deal with his gaslighting?

Yep. And remember how crazy-making it can all be? Remember that life?

Good. Now You Remember Why You Left.

When you feel weak, you have to remember why you left. Or why you're planning to leave.

The gnawing feeling in your stomach when you hear the names you're called or the horrible way he or she seems to see you as a person, maybe.

How your entire being, your character and your integrity were called into question for every little "infraction" of the ridiculous (and often unspoken) rules and double-standards he required of you?

That's why you left. Or maybe it's why you're leaving – or maybe, it's just one reason you can stop crying about the narcissist who left you.

Because now, you are the one who decides what happens. Now it's all about what you want, what you choose, what you say is best.

ABOVE ALL: Don't scare yourself into staying

The narcissist is going to try to make you afraid and insecure. They want you to think you can't live without them and that you can't do better.

Don't let that scare you – I know that being in full control of your life might be a little freaky after having been under someone else's thumb for awhile, but you will very quickly find yourself feeling light and happy in a way that you can't remember feeling before.

You can do better. I don't care if your overweight or you're frumpy or you're very, very shy – no one deserves the mental and emotional abuse of a narcissist. It's pure torture and you can do better.

Know that. And remind yourself when you feel weak. You can do this. You can be who you want, and you can take care of yourself. KNOW IT!

Change is hard but you will come out so much happier and more fulfilled.

While your initial reaction to any sort of change is going to be difficult sometimes, this is especially true when it involves separation from someone you've spent many years or even months with.

That's because a lot of times, you literally sort of forget who you are – you've become so enmeshed and codependent with your narcissist that you literally don't know who you'd be without him.

REMEMBER: Your situation and what you're dealing with now doesn't make you wrong, less than anyone else or stupid; it makes you human.

People who have not experienced the hell of narcissistic abuse in a toxic relationship have absolutely no idea how incredibly it takes over everything in your life.

Before you know it, you are literally putting every single word you say and choice you make through the "narcissist filter," which is your understanding of what will and will not upset the narcissist.

Removing the "Narcissist Filter" From Your Self-Identity

So now that you've made the choice to leave, it's time to begin to shed the narcissist's version of you and start to create your own perfect version – what you consider the be the best possible version of yourself.

If that means you need to spend a bit of time getting over your relationship first, fine – but set a time limit and stick to it.

And then, you can get on about the business of deciding who you are after you end a relationship with a narcissist.

CHAPTER 24: REDEFINE YOURSELF AFTER A TOXIC RELATIONSHIP

"Travel deep inside yourself without the baggage of conditioning. Be an explorer, have patience and eventually your true nature will surface. You will return from your journey with fresh skin and you will approach each day with a wonderful sense of wonder and bliss." ~Marco R. Capristo

Whether we recognize it or not, most everyone's habits and behavior are a result of some form of conditioning – and for those who have experienced the painful and all-encompassing abuse that a narcissist is known for, the conditioning hasn't always been in our best interest.

It begins when we're small children–our parents' opinions of us begin to help us form our own perceptions of ourselves. If we're cursed with narcissistic parents, our perceptions are skewed, twisted…often, plain wrong.

That's because children are sponges – they absorb everything in their environment, including and especially the opinions of their parents and other prominent people in their lives.

If they tell us we're beautiful, we believe that we are–but if they tell us we're horrible and sick, we'll believe that too.

And it doesn't end there–add in the opinions of your teachers, siblings and friends…and later those of your spouse, your bosses and coworkers, neighbors and don't forget that lady at the dry cleaner's last week.

All of this "conditioning," left unchecked, can sometimes add up to a very negative self-image–especially if you don't know that you don't have to accept it. And, we become what we perceive–we are what we believe we are.

Here's the thing, friend. I've been saying this for years, and I don't mean to nag. But please, take just a second and really focus on this next sentence.

You don't have to accept someone else's judgment, perception or opinion of you. You get to write your own story. You feel me? But seriously, go back and read it one more time if you need to – it's that important.

Fact is, you can be whomever and whatever you choose. All you have to do is believe that you can–really believe it. I mean, feel it down to your bones. And then, believe that you're receiving it, that you've already received it. Own it–because it's yours if you want it.

Bliss Mission: Choose Your Own Story

Today, I challenge you to take a look at the people around you–those you love, those you like and even those who present certain struggles. Remember your childhood, and the people you spent time with during that time.

Now, think of all the perceptions they had about you. Your parents? Your friends? Others?

Then, think about you. Have you adopted someone else's opinion of who you are? Or have you constantly struggled against it? Do you feel guilty for being who you are, because you haven't become what someone else wanted you to become?

Most of us can identify with this feeling on some level, I suspect, but most especially those who have been negatively affected by a narcissist's gaslighting and abuse in relationships.

This next part is the hardest part of all, so I hope you're sitting down.

It's time to begin to release the negative self-perceptions you've held on to for years.

BREATHE! This is going to FEEL very difficult, but once you realize how much better your life is going to be, you're going to wonder why you've waited so long. Are you ready for this?

It's finally time to let go of every disapproving look, veiled insult and rude comment.

It's time to wash away the well-intentioned but misguided attempts to save (read: change to fit someone else's idea of perfect) your soul, your sense of fashion and your sense of justice.

I know what you're thinking. Probably something along the lines of "Yeah, sure, and how would you propose I go about THAT?" Well, you know me –

I've got an answer. And, if you know me well, you know that it works –
because it's how I survived my own narcissistic abuse situation.

Try this.

Today, every time you have a negative thought about yourself, take notice
and change your mind.

Cancel the thought, and intentionally replace it with an affirmation of your
true desires. So, if you think to yourself, "I am always late," notice it. Then,
mentally cancel the thought and affirm, "I am always on time."

Perception is everything, my friend. And you can change yours at will. Good
stuff, yes? I think so. Here's a thought to get your wheels turning as you
begin to release any negative perceptions you've held about yourself.

*"The trick is in what one emphasizes. We either make ourselves miserable, or
we make ourselves strong. The amount of work is the same." ~ Carlos
Castaneda*

Do not allow the simplicity of this tip make you doubt its power – this is one
of those things that WORKS – changing your perception intentionally, and
with a little practice, not only will you see results fast, but you'll soon realize
how much control you really DO have over your own life.

CHAPTER 25: THE MIRACLE QUESTION TAKES YOU TO THE NEXT LEVEL

"You've done it before and you can do it now. See the positive possibilities. Redirect the substantial energy of your frustration and turn it into positive, effective, unstoppable determination." ~Ralph Marston

In my life coach certification classes, I learned a really cool technique called "The Miracle Question" that you can use to figure out exactly what you want in life – or at least to more clearly define a goal.

So, when a client is in my office or in an online session and we're trying to figure out what direction to take our time together, I'll ask The Miracle Question.

The Miracle Question: "What if you woke up tomorrow morning and found that a miracle had happened and life was perfect? Your goals have all been met and everything is ideal. What does that look like?"

That question often leaves a person stumped, partially because it's so hard to imagine waking up to such a miracle. And so, I help them dig into even the smallest details of their version of their perfect life – starting with nice, bite-sized pieces.

The Miracle Question in Bite-Sized Pieces

What would you choose to do in your life if you could not be stopped?

Take a few minutes to consider how you would live your life if you had everything you needed.

Would you:

- Go back to school?
- Start your own company?
- Become a philanthropist?
- Buy your own island?

Without limits to your resources, there aren't limits to your options. So, you'd better think big, my friend.

I've found in my coaching practice, as well as in my own life, that this simple exercise can be an excellent way to determine your life's purpose.

If all obstacles were removed and there was literally nothing and no one standing in your way, what would you choose to do?

- Who would be in your life?
- Would you be alone or married?
- How many friends would you have?
- Describe your friends.
- Describe your neighbors.
- How many children would you have?
- If you dream of owning your own business, describe your employees and clients.
- Where would you live?
- Would you stay put or move to the beach?
- How many homes would you own?
- What color would your dining room be?
- Consider the geographical location and the actual dwelling. There are hundreds of castles for sale at any time. You'll need a butler, though.
- What would your typical day be like?
- What time would you get out of bed?
- What would you do first?
- How would you spend your day?
- How would your evening be spent?
- How much free time would you have and how would you spend it?
- Who would you see?
- Would you play golf every Thursday?
- Would you race cars on the weekend?

Okay, so now you know exactly what you want to do – and for the record, in case you weren't clear, that's exactly what you should be doing.

But remember – knowledge is only power when you apply it. So what can you do to make it happen?

Regardless of the current state of your resources, there's always a first step toward your goal that you can take – and a second, third and so on. Each step will help build toward the next. Eventually, you'll baby step your way there.

COACH TIP: The first step might be as simple as finding out what kind of educational opportunities you've got around you, deciding to look for a better or higher-paying job that either gets you closer to your ultimate goal or helps you fund it. Who knows? Maybe it's not too late for you to become the rock star you've always wanted to be – is it time to sign up for those guitar lessons?

With every step, your understanding of the situation and your resources to help fund and/or facilitate it will grow.

Celebrity Inspiration: Just consider billionaire Warren Buffett. Did you know that his humble beginnings in the business world started with a simple paper route?

Now he's often noted as the richest man in the world – or at least one of them.

Good news – most likely, you're already past the whole paper route thing – and your dreams might not be quite as lofty as becoming the richest man in the world. So, what does that mean? Well, you can SOOOOO totally do this. Yep. It is, in fact, scientifically possible.

Fake It Til You Make It!

Like just about anything else in life, you can sort of change your perception now and watch your reality go with it. So, if you can sort of "pretend "you have unlimited resources, then you can start to find solutions to challenges.

By imagining you have nothing standing in your way, you can open your mind to all the possible solutions.

Maybe you will find a solution that requires additional resources but give yourself a chance to make it work. Turn obstacles into opportunity! Those with unlimited resources can still struggle, so having unlimited resources isn't a guarantee- it's all about how you see it.

Focus on the abundance in the world and never forget that that many of the most successful people in the world started at the very bottom with not even a couple of nickels to rub together.

Believing that nothing can stand in your way and living in accord can help to determine your life's purpose, your dream existence, and create a new set of solutions. Imagining that your resources are plentiful will open new possibilities.

It is time to stop limiting yourself, my friend. What would you do with unlimited resources? What would you do if you were UNSTOPPABLE?

CHAPTER 27: STOP APOLOGIZING AND START DOING NICE THINGS FOR YOURSELF

Until just a few years ago, I rarely found a justifiable reason to do anything nice for myself - and if I did, I felt like I had to sneak around and find a way to hide it from everyone. I felt like I was doing something wrong. Sadly, this isn't uncommon for survivors of narcissistic abuse - we feel like we need to apologize or like we're being selfish when we spend a little money on ourselves, or when we just give ourselves a break.

Do you feel guilty when you do something just for yourself? I know I used to - I would always be apologizing! But not anymore.

Many of us feel like we can't do something nice for ourselves without feeling that old familiar pang of guilt. We feel that if we spend time taking care of ourselves, somehow that takes things and time away from our loved ones.

While that's technically true, there are some big benefits in putting yourself first - and you really shouldn't feel guilty about it. When you fly on an airplane, you're instructed to take care of yourself first in a case of emergency, before helping others, including your children.

That point is made for a good reason. If we don't put ourselves first and take care of our own need, we will have a hard time helping others. Does this give us a free pass to become completely selfish? Of course not! But it does mean that we can sneak a few minutes here and there to make ourselves a priority. In fact, as a survivor, you MUST do exactly that - if you're ever going to heal.

What does that mean?

It means we shouldn't run ourselves so ragged that we become sleep deprived, stressed out people who frankly aren't all that fun to be around. You know this deep down. When you take the time to put yourself first and do something selfish for a little while, you come back refreshed and in a much better frame of mind to tackle whatever life throws at you.

Locking yourself in the bedroom and reading a book for an hour doesn't make you a bad person. Taking a mini time-out by playing a silly game on your phone doesn't make you a bad parent. Going out to dinner with your girlfriends doesn't make you a bad person. Instead, it makes you better at what you do. You're ready to figure out how to budget for the new washing machine you need to buy after you've taken a little break.

You feel me? GIVE YOURSELF A BREAK!

You're better and more focused at your job after taking the weekend completely off work. You're calmer and steadier after you've had a chance to vent your frustration over the toothpaste, the toilet lid, and the dirty laundry on the floor. You're a better and more patient parent who will gladly read the same book for the 50th time after you unwound playing candy crush for a few minutes.

Say it with me now: I WILL NOT APOLOGIZE FOR TAKING CARE OF MYSELF!!

All I want you to do is this: Stop feeling guilty about taking the time to care for yourself, relax and unwind. It makes you a much better person and I'm sure your loved ones want you to be calm, relaxed, and happy. It's time to stop the guilt and go do something fun just for yourself. One little thing. And do not apologize for it.

Visit QueenBeeing.com/selfcare for a free self-care toolbox.

CHAPTER 28: THE BEST REVENGE ON THE NARCISSIST

Have you ever wished you could get back at the narcissist in your life? Or make them pay for what they've done? If so, you're most definitely not alone!

I've been hearing a lot of survivors tell me they really want to figure out a way to get revenge for what a narcissist has done to them and their lives - or at least to be able to hold them accountable. Really, what I think they want is some kind of closure. Either way, they're frustrated - and who can blame them? After all, narcissists really do a number on our lives - they destroy our self-esteem and take our very identities from us in so many ways. So, what can we do to sort of get back at them?

It seems to be part of human nature to want revenge. We like the idea of justice. Whether we suffered at the hands of a cruel and incompetent boss or were treated badly and dumped by a toxic partner, we want our pound of flesh. And while that's understandable since narcissists never leave us with closure, it turns out that this approach is flawed for several reasons:

- You're spending your time on someone who doesn't care about you as an individual (narcissistic supply doesn't count!).
- You can create serious challenges for yourself if you take things too far.
- You let them off the hook. Once you strike back, they have the luxury of "knowing" they were right to mistreat you. It gives a narcissist "justification" for their continued abuse.

Though it seems less exciting than publicly humiliating the narcissist or building a car bomb (lol!), living a great life is actually an effective way to get revenge.

Try these techniques to get revenge by living the best life you can:

Live every moment with intention. Simply becoming aware of how you're spending your time can help - but it's more than awareness. Stop wasting your time and energy on people who don't deserve it. Start spending more time with people who are worth your energy - even if that begins with just yourself.

Find and follow your passion! Find an activity that's meaningful to you. Figure out what it is that sets your soul on fire! This is one of the best ways to not only keep yourself busy, but to do so in a meaningful way that can positively affect your life in ways you may not be able to imagine yet! Not sure what gets you going? Go pick up my free passion finder at QueenBeeing.com/passion. A life with more meaning is more fulfilling on a personal level. When you're doing something that's meaningful to you, you have a glow that other people can't resist.

Enhance your health and fitness. There's a reason why so many men and women manage to finally lose weight after going through a break-up. It's a great thing to do for yourself. It also feels good to show everyone that you really are better without the narcissist in your life!

Build your social circle. Get some new friends and/or reconnect with old ones. Fact: Increasing the size and quality of your social circle is a wonderful way to take your life to the next level. The narcissist will cringe at your new level of popularity.

Become more influential. Do something BIG! Become a more important person. This can be at work, socially, online, or in your community. How can you become a more powerful person in the world? Even a small improvement in this area is noticeable to others.

Declutter your life. One of the things that can hold you back is all the clutter in your life. It's not just the extra items that you own. It's the low-quality people, obligations, and worries, too. Eliminate all the mediocrity from your life, and your life will blossom.

Are you getting my point yet? The BEST, MOST POWERFUL way to get revenge on a narcissist is to live your life WELL, to be happy and fulfilled WITHOUT the narcissist - despite the fact that they exist, without their influence.

Enjoy your life. Simply go out and enjoy your life to the fullest. It will drive the narcissist nuts - but you won't care, because your life is amazing!

You feel me? Get your revenge by taking your life to the next level.

This is *the* best form of revenge.

Get started on your recovery for free and find free tools and tips for every stage at QueenBeeing.com.

DOMESTIC VIOLENCE EMERGENCY?

Get Real-World Resources for Victims of Physical and Emotional Abuse

If you're being physically abused in any way, you've got to take action now. While emotional abuse can affect you in many ways, including your health, physical abuse should be considered an emergency situation and you should be prepared to do whatever is necessary to ensure your physical safety as quickly as possible.

If you are being physically abused, please get out of the situation ASAP. I'm not being dramatic when I tell you that your life might depend on it.

Find emergency help

If you need help right now, or you've already been hurt, call 911 (or your country's emergency number).

Find advice and support

In **the US**: call the National Domestic Violence Hotline at 1-800-799-7233 (SAFE).

UK: call Women's Aid at 0808 2000 247.

Australia: call 1800RESPECT at 1800 737 732.

Worldwide: visit International Directory of Domestic Violence Agencies for a global list of helplines, shelters, and crisis centers.

Find a safe place to stay

In the US: visit Womenslaw.org for a state-by-state directory of domestic violence shelters in the U.S.

Male victims of abuse can call:

U.S. and Canada: The Domestic Abuse Helpline for Men & Women

UK: ManKind Initiative

Australia: <u>One in Three Campaign</u>

www.ingramcontent.com/pod-product-compliance
Lightning Source LLC
Chambersburg PA
CBHW021006160726
47994CB00006B/2393